SLEEPTALK™

A GIFT OF LOVE THROUGH
POSITIVE PARENTING

Joane Goulding

How to empower your child to achieve
self-confidence and inner strength!

PENNON
PUBLISHING
2004

First published in Australia in 2004 by:
Pennon Publishing
59 Fletcher Street
Essendon Vic 3041
www.pennon.com.au

Text copyright © Joane Goulding

All rights reserved. No part of this book may be reproduced, stored in a retrieval system, or transmitted in any form or by any means electronic, mechanical or otherwise, without the prior written permission of the publisher.

Every effort has been made to ensure that this book is free from error or omissions. However, the publisher, the author and their respective employees or agents, do not accept responsibility for injury, loss or damage occasioned to any person acting or refraining from action as a result of material in this book whether or not such injury, loss or damage is in any way due to any negligent act or omission, breach of duty or default on the part of the publisher, the author, or their respective employees or agents.

The National Library of Australia
Cataloguing-in-Publication entry:

   Goulding, Joane.
      Sleep talk : a gift of love through positive parenting.

      ISBN 1 877029 70 X.

      1. Mental suggestion. 2. Child rearing. 3. Parent and
      child. I. Title.

      649.64

Designed by Allan Cornwell
Printed in China through Bookbuilders

Disclaimer.
The information contained in this book is for educational purposes only. You are advised to consult with your health care professional with regard to matters relating to your health. The authors accept no liability for damages arising from the abuse of the information contained herein.

Dedication

Two precious souls that it has been my privilege to know — my daughters Michelle and Teresa, thank you both for choosing me as your mum. Your journey has been the catalyst for SleepTalk™ and for that I am eternally grateful. Kahlil Gibran the prophet states: 'Your children are not your children, they are the sons and the daughters of life's longing for itself. They come through you but not from you. And though they are with you, yet they belong not to you'.

Acknowledgements

Where and how can I thank so many people who have helped me achieve the completion of this book. So many people have contributed, directly and indirectly, thoughts, ideas and suggestions that it would be impossible for me to thank each one separately. You know who you are, and it has been a pleasure to have known each and every one of you.

The birth of the idea to write this book came in the late 1980s when sitting with friends in front of a warm fire in Mildura one cold winter day, Merv Saultry suggested I write the book and encouraged me to 'just do it'. Thank you Merv for your encouragement and belief in me and the SleepTalk™ process. To my dear friend, Rosemary Hanger, who spent many hours over the following years transcribing my notes into her computer, expertly deciphering my writing: Rosemary, I am eternally grateful. You knew what I was trying to say even when I had difficulty finding the right words. How did you manage to do that? Your patience, support, continued encouragement, but most of all your belief in me, and the friendship you so generously gave has been a precious gift and I thank you. To Noel Odou who edited my first draft: Noel, how on earth did you manage to sort out the jumble of ideas and words that I added into the margins and in-between paragraphs? You even understood (in spite of the spell check) my dyslectic spelling. You understood the emotions that I was experiencing, you gave so generously of your time and I appreciate all the help and advice you offered.

Throughout the past years as SleepTalk™ has become established, so many families, parents and children contributed to the process. To the parents that believed in SleepTalk™, allowed me the privilege of working with you and have allowed me to tell your stories, my grateful thanks. Someone once said that life has a way of producing the right person at the right time. Synchronicity is wonderful isn't it.

To my colleagues and friends that so kindly shared their professional knowledge and expertise, I thank you all. You believed in this process, you encouraged, supported and inspired me to continue my journey and complete this book. Special thanks to Michael Wilson, Dr Portia Reading, Heather Osborne, Sue McDonald, Michelle Stanton, Alan Stubenrauch and Terry Suckling for your professional help and advice. To the colleagues that contributed case histories and shared their experiences, my grateful acknowledgement and thanks. Sharon Clark, Paul Black, Ann Fynmore, Paula Jacobs and Dr Eileen Feeney enabled me to present a deeper understanding of this precious process.

To Sandi Rogers, CEO of the National College of Traditional Medicine I offer my respect and appreciation for your generous comments in the foreword. My grateful thanks to John Cheetham, Director of the Student Achievement Centre, for your encouraging support over the years. To Brian James who assisted me to develop ideas and to Alex Bartsch for your insightful thoughts you so generously shared when writing the preface, thank you. To Elaine Stoeckel, my adopted sister, your contribution and sharing of nutritional knowledge has given us all food for thought. To my publisher and sometimes counsellor Bev Friend, who encouraged me, picked me up when times were very difficult, who believed in me and the SleepTalk ™ process, and who gave me this opportunity to share my thoughts with you, just saying thank you seems somehow insignificant.

To my late husband Jim Goulding: Jim you died in 2001 before this book was completed. Without your support, inspiration and unique ability to understand the creative principles of the mind this precious process called SleepTalk™ would not exist. Thank you for your generous spirit, your love and support and above all for just being you. Finally to the beautiful souls who have shared my journey, my daughters Michelle and Teresa, I offer my deep love and respect. It has been an honour and privilege to be your mother and friend.

Children live by what they learn.
If a child lives with criticism, they learn to condemn.
If a child lives with hostility, they learn to fight.
If a child lives with ridicule, they learn to be shy.
If a child lives with shame, they learn to be guilty.
If a child lives with tolerance, they learn to be patient.
If a child lives with encouragement, they learn confidence.
If a child lives with praise, they learn to appreciate.
If a child lives with fairness, they learn justice.
If a child lives with security, they learn to have faith.
If a child lives with approval, they learn to like themselves.
If a child lives with acceptance and friendship,
they learn to find love in the world.

author unknown

Children are our future, and as parents
we need to recognise this with a sense of urgency.
If we are to take care of our children's future,
we need to take care of the 'now'.
Remember it's not what we leave to our children
that matters, it's what we leave within their minds.

Joane Goulding

Contents

About the author

As an educator for some 30 years, with extensive experience in stress management and nutrition, Joane has specialised in the biopsychosocial aspect of stress and mind management. She has published many papers and lectured throughout Australia and in the USA, and is a member of numerous professional organisations. Her background covers many distinct pathways.

Throughout her professional career Joane has been involved in psycho-nutrition, education, training and coaching. For 22 years Joane was Director of the Australian Academy of Hypnotic Science. In 1998 the Academy became a national and international government accredited private provider of education and an accredited training organisation. Joane authored the documentation relating to registration as a private provider of education and authored the *Hypnosis Training Manual*. The Academy offered certificates in Communication and Counselling, Conflict Resolution and a Diploma of Health — Clinical Hypnosis.

In 1998 Joane was awarded a fellowship for services to the science of hypnosis by the Australian Society of Clinical Hypnotherapists which acknowledged her contribution to the science of hypnosis and changes to the Victorian *Psychological Practices Act*. An approved supervisor, mentor and lecturer in the hypnosis industry, Joane is also a master hypnotist, lecturer and examiner for the American Council of Hypnotic Examiners. She is a qualified psycho-nutritionalist and innovator of numerous psycho-nutritional diagnostic questionnaires and procedures and was in private practice for many years.

The English *International Biographical Directory 1987* records Joane was awarded a 'Distinguished Achievement' award and the American Biographical Institute recognised her 'Outstanding Service to the Healing Profession'.

Throughout her professional life, one of Joane's goals was to develop SleepTalk™ for Children. As the innovator and author of SleepTalk™ for Children, Joane's objective has been to reach as many children as possible and assist them by using the process called SleepTalk™. This process enables all children, whether they are normal, gifted or in need of extra assistance to benefit from this special gift.

Parents' involvement with the development and wellness of their children is paramount in today's society. Inculcated belief patterns and historically accepted modes of behaviour are passed down through generations. SleepTalk™ grew out of the experience Joane had with her own daughter Michelle, who was diagnosed as having an intellectual and emotional IQ of 45 at the age of seven and suffering from cerebral palsy and severe learning difficulties. Her passion to do the absolute best for her daughter led to the discovery of techniques that dramatically improved the condition of her child beyond all expectation.

SleepTalk™ for Children is an enlightened and practical process of assisting children to maximise their individual potential. It is based on the fundamental principles of how the human mind and brain function. SleepTalk™ assists parents to create an environment in which a child's self-esteem and confidence grow and flourish and as a consequence reinforce, or if necessary re-establish, a positive attitude to life. The process enhances a child's ability to take control of their thinking and decision making, to develop attitudes which will promote their quality of life.

SleepTalk™ instils resilience within the child, and gives them the confidence to say 'NO'. The SleepTalk™ process takes only a few moments of the parent's time each evening, with positive feedback of change expected within 21 days. For parents who wish to further their involvement with SleepTalk™ an option to become a licensed coach is available.

Joane's philosophy:

Children are our future, it is their right to develop and grow in a happy, harmonious and positive mental environment. Parents and society in general should give every child the opportunity to develop to their full independent potential. The SleepTalk™ process helps dreams and goals to be obtained and to establish within a child a positive, confident self-image. When a child has a basic belief in self and achieves harmony with their environment the world becomes their 'oyster' and achievement beyond imagination is possible. We need to recognise this with a sense of urgency.

If we are to take care of our children's future, we need to take care of the 'now'. Remember it's not what we leave to our children that matters it's what we leave within their minds.

Joane can be contacted at joane1@bigpond.com.au or www.sleeptalk-children.com

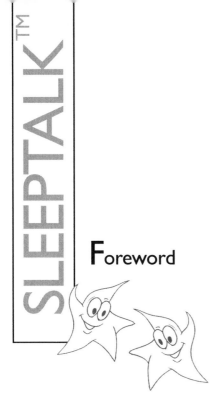

Foreword

THERE IS STRONG EVIDENCE TO SUPPORT such an innovative and timely process as SleepTalk™ for Children. As families face more and more challenges, parents require assistance to engage with their children and form strong bonds, yet at the same time struggle to provide the lifestyle they want for their offspring.

Too often, as children react to these tensions, it is they who are counselled and not the parents. The strength of SleepTalk™ is the relationship that is built with the parents, who then take the process to their child and introduce it in a gentle and guided manner producing astounding results.

SleepTalk™ for Children is one of the most useful tools I have employed in over two decades of being in clinical practice.

Perhaps the most impressive aspect of the process is the way in which Joane considered her ethical obligations to both the clients (parents) and the recipient/s (children).

With every turn of a page integrity, care and ethical boundaries are presented to the reader. This invokes great confidence in the practitioners wishing to use SleepTalk™ for Children in clinical practice as well as those searching for solutions as they grapple with the responsibilities of parenting.

This wonderful and very effective process will become one of the most sought after as communities realise the importance and effectiveness of all forms of communication. The result will be a far more productive and caring community.

Congratulations Joane on presenting this gold mine to parents who can only benefit from it and for the children whose self-esteem will grow; and be the adults of the future.

Sandi B. Rogers MEd, ND, DMH
CEO National College of Traditional Medicine

Testimonials

I have personally used SleepTalk™ for Children for over 20 years. My own two children, Monique and Ren, have grown into adulthood feeling secure and loved, I believe, as a result of this miracle. I continue in my busy practice to use, and educate others, on the wonderful benefits of SleepTalk™ for Children.

Cherie de Haas
Presenter, 'Healthy, Wealthy and Wise', naturopath, author

It is with pleasure that I commend to you the SleepTalk™ program by Joane Goulding.

The SleepTalk™ program is an excellent resource for caring families. It is simple and easy to use for all parents and suits children – from gifted to talented to challenged – to enhance their peace of mind and belief in their abilities.

It empowers parents to give their children positive suggestions to help with general and specific issues in their lives. It aids parents in taking action yet still allows the child to take responsibility for his or her own growth. SleepTalk™ is an invaluable tool for boosting a child's self-esteem.

Dr Janet Hall, MAPsS
Clinical and Counselling Psychologist

6 The Orangery,
Ham Street,
Richmond, Surrey
TW10 7HS
eileen.feeney@totalise.co.uk

May 13, 2002

To: Whom it concerns
Re: SleepTalk™ therapy

Dear Sir or Madam:

I am a qualified medical practitioner and psychiatrist. I have used the technique of SleepTalk™ therapy over the past 14 years. I have found it to be very safe and effective. It has many applications including enhancing the self-esteem of the child, building confidence to go swimming or reading aloud in class, bed-wetting etc. I have received very positive feedback from the parents of the children who were treated.

I have no hesitation in endorsing the credibility of this therapy. I have taught this technique to other medical colleagues. In addition, I have presented at academic meetings case studies of patients who were treated successfully.

This is a very useful therapy. It will be a major step forward to have further information about it published.

I am happy to be contacted if further information is required.

Yours faithfully,

Dr Eileen Feeney
MB, BCh, BAO, BA, DCH, FRANZCP

Jeff Berger
Consulting Psychologist
Scarsdale ,Vic 3351
fax 03 5342 2484

8th May 2002

TO WHOM IT MAY CONCERN

Joane Goulding is the author of a new and innovative book on the concept of SleepTalk™, a self-esteem programme that fosters a sense of confidence, self-assurance and empowerment in children. Practitioners and parents have used SleepTalk™ over many years to assist children in their growth and development.

Having used the principles of SleepTalk™ in my practice as a psychologist, and having trained others to do so as well, I have no doubt that it is a valuable tool in working with children on a number of levels with the challenges of life they may experience from time to time. SleepTalk™ is a positive, natural, non-invasive and non-harmful treatment regime, the benefits of which can literally last forever.

There is no doubt that the time is now right for the benefits of the SleepTalk™ process to be disseminated more widely among healthcare professionals and the general community.

I wholeheartedly support Joane's effort to make SleepTalk™ more widely known. If further information is required I would be happy to give it and I can be contacted on any of the numbers below.

Yours sincerely

Jeffrey A. Berger
BA(Psych), BTH, Grad.Dip. Counselling Psych

Professor Ian E. Brighthope MBBS
Fellow – Australasian College of Nutritional and Environmental
Medicine
PO Box 153 Dingley Vic, 3172
fax 03 9769 1880

Joane Goulding's 'SleepTalk™ therapy' is a sensible, practical and easy-to-follow method of communicating important messages to the subconscious mind. It is especially useful for effecting changes to children's behaviour. By combining nutritional therapies to create an optimum molecular environment with 'SleepTalk™ therapy', a wider range of physical, emotional and neuropsychiatric disorders can be more effectively treated than by standard psychological and medical approaches.

This book should be read by all parents, educators and health professionals and the practice adopted in the management of all disorders in which the mind plays a significant role.

Professor Ian E. Brighthope
MBBS, Dip Ag Sci,FACNEM, FASEM, MAIAST

Teya Antonia-Wright
Author and trainer. Born to be Free.

As a mother and transformational therapist it has been my privilege to endorse SleepTalk™ for Children. Many years ago I had an opportunity to work with this unique process to assist my daughter, Alicia, after I had seen Joane working with her own daughter Michelle. I was so moved emotionally to see the changes in Michelle that I worked with Joane in regard to the procedure. My goal was to have my little girl cope with being emotionally traumatised by the break-up of my marriage to her father. As a direct result of working with the SleepTalk™ process the happy, less confused little girl that greeted me each day was testimony that this very simple process was powerful beyond measure. SleepTalk™ for Children transferred Alicia from an emotionally traumatised child to a happy and bright little girl. If you would like more information please feel free to contact me at www.TeyaInc.com.

Teya Antonia-Wright
Dip Nut, Sc, Dip Psychotherapy

SLEEPTALK™

Preface — Alex Bartsch*, BA Hons Psych

The power of words — your gift to your child

'Sticks and stones may break my bones, but words will never hurt me?' So why is it that the pen is mightier than the sword? Because words have the power to build or destroy, comfort or hurt. Words convey information that is processed and then accepted or rejected depending on the foundations of our subconscious belief system.

So... how do you view your world? Is it a dangerous place, full of obstacles, hardship, threats, and misfortune? An experience to be endured? Or is your world an exciting and inviting place, where opportunities for learning and development abound, and living is mainly pleasurable? Why is it that while we all inhabit the same physical world, there are vast differences in our perceptions of it? Our realities are as unique as our bodies. Every single one a 'genuine original'.

---

*Alex Bartsch is a director of Zenith Professional Development and a registered psychologist. Contact details are in the Recommended Reading chapter.

What if you had the opportunity to give your child a lifelong gift? A gift that enables your child to overcome obstacles, recognise opportunities, and maximise their potential for success. A creative gift that allows your child to build the foundations that facilitate a positive attitude to their world, and takes only five minutes of your time each night!

The critical years in your child's development

We are all born with a certain potential that is dictated by our genes. Whether or not we fulfil that potential is significantly affected by the amount and KIND of stimulation we receive in the early years of our lives.

Social scientists have long suspected that children's intelligence and well-being are affected by their environment — whether or not they are nourished adequately, challenged intellectually, and given enough affection. Now, modern brain-imaging techniques have confirmed this notion. According to Professor William Greenough of the University of Illinois, the actual physical wiring of the brain is susceptible to experience. But perhaps the most significant news concerns the impact of a baby's environment on the development of his or her brain.

It is in the first years of your child's life that the brain undergoes enormous physical changes as it builds its personal 'wiring' system, incorporating a number of systems or programs that facilitate function, survival and development. This wiring consists of an incredibly large number of connections known as synapses, which are formed as a result of stimuli that cause electrical and chemical activity in the brain. The amount and type of stimulation that a child receives dictates the number, and combinations of connections that are made. These connections are strengthened through further stimulation and use. In fact the foundational networking of the brain's synapses is nearly complete after the rapid brain development of the first three years.

Brief but golden opportunity

As the first few years are critical to brain development, parents have a brief but golden opportunity to help stimulate and form the brain circuitry of their children, laying the foundations for the development of effective cognitions and beliefs that are critical in determining a child's responses to the world around it. Researchers in the field of early childhood development have also made discoveries that provide parents with guiding principles for encouraging development.

Firstly, infants have a biological need and desire to learn. Therefore they are completely open to experience, and actively seek stimulation. This means that you can increase the volume and complexity of your child's brain circuitry by providing it with stimulating experiences, which can also provide the foundations for enhanced learning in the future. The 'Foundation' processes of SleepTalk™ provides this essential element. In fact the amount of connections in the brain can fluctuate by as much as 25% depending on the type of stimulation and environment a child is exposed to.

Although visual stimulation can produce developmental advantages including enhanced curiosity, attentiveness and concentration, any type of basic interaction with your child is beneficial. It is during the first few months that the brain's wiring is fine-tuned, and excess cells and synapses — typically those that have never been used — are eliminated, according to Dr Kathryn Taaffe-Young, a developmental psychologist who has extensively researched the importance of maximising the learning potential of children prior to the age of three. Dr Taaffe-Young maintains that the first year is critical for healthy brain development and that if synapses aren't used, they die, with no chance of revival.

What this means is that children reared in environments where stimulation is limited actually have fewer synapses than those raised in environments where they are regularly talked to, held, and visually stimulated, according to Dr Young. You may not have realised it, but all of the things that you do with your baby regularly add up: when you sing to an infant, talk to her, hold her, play with her, and give her appropriate toys and objects to explore, you are creating an environment that enables her brain to develop to its maximum potential.

Every child has a real need for attention and affection. Babies do not try to control their parents' lives; they simply have a biological need for interaction with them. Providing affection and attending to a baby's needs creates an environment that is stable, secure and comforting. This is a perfect platform on which to build positive and effective thought patterns that are critical in determining healthy levels of self-esteem and self-efficacy in the future.

The most effective practical strategies

What then, are the most effective practical strategies that parents can employ to create an appropriate environment for their children?

First, talk to your baby often with a kind voice, a wide range of vocabulary, and a lot of expression. Your voice is one of your child's favourite sounds. It is familiar and comforting. Remember, it has been hearing the sound of your voice since it was *in utero*!

Second, respond to your child's requests. This teaches the child that it can communicate with other people and gives it a strong sense of trust and emotional stability.

Third, touch your child as often as possible. Premature infants who are massaged grow faster, cry less, and are released earlier from the hospital than those who aren't. Appropriate touching encourages a sense of security and comfort in children.

Last, but by no means least, teach your baby through your own model of appropriate and positive behaviour. Encourage your child to imitate your positive, supportive and comforting gestures. Verbalise your positive feelings towards them, and reinforce these phrases with complementary actions. Your baby is constantly observing and analysing your behaviour and working out ways to mimic your voice and facial expressions.

One of the goals of SleepTalk™ is to improve the human thought stream, the running mental commentary that accompanies us through life as we observe, compare and judge events going on around us.

While there are some things in our lives that we will never be able to control, the vast majority of what happens to us is directly affected by — us! Many of us have been taught that good things happen to people who do good, and that if we do 'the right thing', we will be rewarded. So why don't we always get rewarded? Why do terrible things happen to people who do 'the right thing'? Why do some people live in a state of perpetual anxiety? Why do others appear to glide through life without any apparent care?

The answer, to a great extent, lies in the fact that our BELIEFS about things and events determine our reactions and behaviours towards them. If children consciously or unconsciously believe that they will 'never be any good at school', are 'unattractive to others', or 'will never amount to anything in life', the chances are they will act out those beliefs and make them a reality. It is a self-fulfilling prophecy. Fortunately, the opposite can also be true. Those with a positive outlook, who display traits such as patience, tolerance, confidence, flexibility, and self-efficacy, tend to cope relatively well with the obstacles life throws up. Just as in the case of infants discussed earlier, children, adolescents and adults also form their personal beliefs from the 'programming' they get from the world around them.

How can we take control of our lives and make them what we want them to be? One way is by 'reprogramming' the way we interpret events around us, both through conscious and unconscious techniques. Through a process such as SleepTalk™, the power of the spoken word, presented in an appropriate format, ensures that the child internalises and appropriates desirable and effective beliefs about his/her place in the world. Once these thoughts have been internalised, the child will not allow him/herself, or anyone else for that matter, to tell them they are not capable, or any other limiting statements that have been made throughout their lives.

Children can discard negative and self-defeating statements
By hearing enough examples of positive and effective thoughts, delivered by a person with whom the child enjoys a close and loving

relationship, the child can eventually discard negative feelings and self-defeating statements and replace them with powerful and useful ones. In this sense SleepTalk™ shares many parallels with a well-recognised psychological therapeutic approach known as self-instruction or self-verbalisation. It might be said that where the two approaches differ is that SleepTalk™ focuses on the use of the sub-conscious, while self-instruction concentrates on the conscious.

Benefits of SleepTalk™

The beauty of the SleepTalk™ process is its simplicity, both in content and delivery. With appropriate training, parents can convey to their children sentences that deliver suitable beliefs and life-strategies. Furthermore, as children are repeatedly exposed to positive language in the process, thoughts and beliefs embed themselves into the child's system of beliefs. Therefore, the process can be used to train and build confidence, self-esteem and self-management. Children who possess appropriate and positive belief systems experience less frustration; they possess a greater range of coping mechanisms and statements. The real power of the process is that once the desirable thoughts and behaviours are in place, they are constantly being used, even in small and subtle ways.

Eventually, the positive system of thoughts and beliefs become an 'ingrained habit', instigating non-conscious life-long changes in behaviour.

What then are the practical benefits of this powerful process of positive parenting that create a safeguard against negative cognitive inoculation? A number of longitudinal studies on the effects of children's belief systems on both their physical and mental health have delivered interesting and compelling findings. For example, children with negative explanatory styles of events are more likely to suffer from reactive depression, low achievement and physical illness, than those with positive styles (Gillham, J.E. & Reivich, K.J., 1999). Furthermore, children who display high levels of pessimism and passivity are at greater risk of chronic depression, and suffering elevated incidence of chronic illnesses in middle to late adulthood.

Interestingly, children whose explanatory styles were changed through therapy suffered fewer repeat episodes of depression than those whose styles did not change (Gillham, J.E., Reivich, K.J., Jaycox, L. & Seligman, M.E.P., 1995).

The good news is that research indicates that negative explanatory styles can be altered and even eliminated through processes such as SleepTalk™.

The five minute gift that lasts a lifetime

The greatest legacy anyone can leave their child, regardless of financial or social status, is a belief system that allows them to effectively deal with all aspects of their world. SleepTalk™ allows parents to complement their existing support strategies with a process that is inexpensive, efficient and effective.

In order to maximise the potential of our children's development, we must be prepared to allow our innate sense of curiosity to guide our judgement. SleepTalk™ does challenge the conventional boundaries of what is considered 'normal' or 'familiar'. However, it is the need to explore our world, create and absorb change, and continually seek more effective ways of developing, that sets us apart as a species; it is the reason we are the pre-eminent organism on the planet, enjoying a level of comfort and control of our environment, unparalleled in history.

The challenges presented by SleepTalk™ are not meant to be overcome in the short-term and then discarded. They can form the foundation of an ongoing, life-long process designed to facilitate and accelerate personal growth and learning. Hopefully, the changes made through SleepTalk™ will be passed on to generations to come, in the hope that the attitudes and belief systems they build become sufficient and necessary elements of a successful and fulfilled life.

Imagine the effect of this aim. Happier and healthier individuals, both physically and psychologically, capable of building societies in which people routinely act with integrity, honesty, tolerance, confidence and flexibility. Do you think this impossible? It is not.

The process of giving and receiving positive messages creates an atmosphere of support. Nothing is impossible if you have the right support. If the sentiments expressed in the preceding pages have struck a chord with you, please read on.

When you think positive, happy, loving thoughts, there's a different chemistry that goes into your body than when you think negative, anguished thoughts. The way you decide to think has a dramatic effect on your chemistry and your physiology.
Wayne W. Dyer

chapter one

Introduction to SleepTalk™

CONTAINED IN THIS BOOK ARE SECRETS SO SIMPLE it's a tragedy that everyone doesn't know them, and so powerful that it's not outlandish to describe the results as miracles. If you could whisper in your child's ear, 'Your life will be wonderful and happy' and make it happen, wouldn't you call it a miracle?

This book is for every parent who wants their children to reach their potential — whatever that potential may be. It is for children with difficulties and for children with none. In other words, it is for your child. It is not about 'curing' conditions but it is about making the most of what 'is'. It is about fertilising your child's mind with the power of the positive, of giving your child the greatest gift of all — an attitude of happiness and confident self-esteem and that, no matter what, they are loved and lovable.

The techniques used in SleepTalk™ for Children are simple and take only a few moments each day. However, importantly, all the considerations which arose as the process was developed are also discussed, enabling you to understand and feel comfortable about the process before starting to work with your child.

I know that this simple yet dynamic self-help process will excite you as much as it has me. I'm sharing it with you in the hope that you will be able to assist your child as I was able to help mine. Expect a 'miracle'. You will have to work for it and you have to want it from the deepest levels of your heart and the most profound thought in your mind, but you can make it happen. From one parent to another, please accept it with my love, empathy and deep understanding.

Benefits of this powerful process of positive parenting

The benefits of SleepTalk™ are not only profound and far reaching to you and your child, but to other areas of life as well. There is, of course, first and foremost, the benefits to your child; then, you the parents, your family, your child's learning environment, and even your working environment.

Benefits for our children

The increased awareness and belief of being loved leads to greater self-esteem, a more positive attitude generally and a sense of empowerment of being able to do things better. Our children become more socially acceptable, and less vulnerable to negative influences by peers. A closer relationship develops, and whatever problem or issue there may have been usually disappears or decreases dramatically.

Benefits as parents

As well as being able to help our children resolve their problems, SleepTalk™ empowers us as parents to contribute to our child's upbringing more effectively; we have a more harmonious and better relationship with our children. The closer involvement with our children provides invaluable learning for parents.

Our children become less demanding, saving time for busy households. More importantly, we are more confident about our parenting, are able to express emotions more openly, and become more aware of the importance of emotions, all of which leads to more relaxed and less stressful life. Improved health and behaviour may also result in saving money and time, which for many families is important.

Benefits for the family

The family, as a unit, becomes a more harmonious and cohesive whole. Communication becomes more open, and relationships are more loving. Being a happier environment for everybody, the family will be able to deal with issues and concerns more effectively, leading to a more cooperative and enjoyable time together. Very importantly, the improved family relations model to all children, not only your child and your family, patterns of relating that will be used in their own parenting and dealing with other adults in their later life, thereby changing social patterns in general.

Learning environment

The overall increased self-esteem resulting from this powerful process of positive parenting has tremendous beneficial effects on children's ability to learn. Improved school results are not only better for your child but more pleasing for you the parents and, of course, the teachers. The benefits of improved school work in turn have a positive effect on the school social life which in itself results in improved behaviour generally. The benefits of SleepTalk™ extend further to other children at school and the teachers, not to mention the character of the school itself.

Work environment

Parents whose children have less issues or concerns are able to be more productive and effective at work as well. The stress of modern work can be reduced when the family situation is improved and less distracted by the challenges of earning a living or pursuing a career. Some work environments are more sensitive to family needs than others, but some do not welcome the burden of family problems. When the issues related to home can be reduced, energy and focus can be devoted to the task, which serves the need of the employees as well as the organisation. SleepTalk™ is a very powerful process of positive parenting and is essential 'must have' knowledge for every family.

If you can imagine it, you can achieve it.
If you can dream it, you can become it.
William Arthur Ward

SLEEPTALK™

chapter two

The story of Michelle. How it all began

THE MORNING OF MICHELLE'S WEDDING HAD ARRIVED and even at this early hour I could tell it was going to be a glorious day. The wedding dress was spread out across the bed, the bridesmaids' flowers, still in their boxes, filled the room with perfume and the family car, washed and resplendent with white ribbon, waited ceremoniously outside. The speeches were prepared and the cake decorated. All was ready for a day I had hardly dared hope would happen.

The household was yet to wake so I made a well-earned cup of coffee and created a little private space for myself before the business of the day took over. As the birds began their early morning chorus I sat on the porch to watch the sun rise and reflect on how my dreams had made this day possible.

Those dreams had enabled me to deal with the terrible distress and heartache which began not long after the birth of my beautiful daughter, Michelle. They were the dreams which let me forget, just for a little while, that Michelle was brain damaged, that she was intellectually impaired, had only basic survival skills and that her speech was affected. They were the dreams which kept me going during many years of relentless pursuit for answers from doctors, psychologists and anyone else who might be able to tell me what was wrong and what I could do about it.

My dreams gave me hope of a happy independent life for my child. They were the same dreams other parents have for their children — of a life of happiness, love and fulfilment — and although at times terribly discouraged, deep down I knew that I would find a way to make these things possible for Michelle.

As I continued to reminisce, allowing my thoughts to float further back in time, I began to relive the terrible confusion and frustration I felt in the early days.

I knew something was wrong; Michelle was not developing as she should. Why didn't anybody else seem concerned? 'There is nothing wrong with your child … she is just slow for her age … don't be such a worrier … she'll be fine … just give her time…' Although desperate to believe the professionals, I knew my child was not the same as others.

Six years later I was still trying to find an explanation for Michelle's 'difference', though now I was dealing with the expert opinion that *I* was 'Michelle's only problem' and that there was 'nothing wrong with Michelle that good parenting couldn't correct'. My feelings of inadequacy and despair were overwhelming.

Michelle was eventually diagnosed with cerebral palsy. Her IQ was approximately 45; she was emotionally disturbed and suffered speech impairment due to dyspraxia of the throat. I felt as if I was drowning in a confusion of emotions. I was at once shocked, devastated, angry and relieved. After years of trying to be a 'better' mother, wearing the guilt of inadequacy and not knowing how to do it any differently, at least I now knew that I had not created this terrible problem for my little girl. I now knew that perhaps there was some way we could manage her condition now that it had an official 'label'.

My determination to find a way became more focused as I listened to the doctors' advice with regard to 'managing' Michelle. I was not going to allow Michelle to be sedated and housed in an institution because her behaviour was unsociable. What could I do to calm her anger, to assist her to learn to walk properly, to help her speak and cry and laugh like other children? I don't know how I knew, but it was clear to me that the way to tackle this problem was to somehow change her deep sense of 'I'm not OK', and to give her a feeling of real worth.

The dream of my daughter finding happiness and being able to live her life independently became my obsession. I created this dream as if I was painting a picture, adding things as they seemed right. In this painting Michelle talked and walked, she ran without falling over, her world was happy and loving … and she experienced the joy of love and marriage. Gradually, as I worked out strategies, those dreams became definitive, confident and purposeful.

The process I have developed, which you will learn in this book, was made possible because my need was great, my determination was mighty and I had wonderful help from two mentors. One was Michelle's stepfather, my husband Jim, who believed passionately in the power of the mind and its creative mechanism. The other was the author of a slim little book simply called *How to Practice Suggestion and Auto Suggestion* by Emile Coué. The realisation that it might be possible for my dreams to come true was one of the most profound experiences of my life. Dreams, make believe and imagination are the first steps towards realisation.

I refused to believe that there was no help for Michelle and started to ask 'what if?' I rejected the negative suggestions of the professionals and as I planned and investigated alternatives, I activated the oldest law of the mind:

If you can imagine it … You can become it.

The procedure that became perfected over a period of two years was so simple, yet so dynamic, it changed our entire world.

Yes, I made mistakes and was sometimes fearful of failure, but as I learned from the mistakes and refined the procedure, I was rewarded with a 'miracle'. It was once said, over 2000 years ago:

'Whatever you believe deepest in your heart it will be afforded unto you'.

Despite the result of the SleepTalk™ process Michelle still had an IQ of only 45 and had to deal with the physical impairments of cerebral palsy and dyspraxia. However, Michelle now had the most precious gift I could ever give her, the belief that … she was loved … she was lovable … she could walk … she could talk … and that life was happy. Her deep subconscious belief that 'I am OK', that life is happy, regardless of individual circumstances, became the foundation of Michelle's world.

The belief that 'I love me, and you're OK too' became the controls which directed her conscious mind. Michelle developed a positive 'I'm OK' attitude which has never let her down.

As I sat with my coffee the morning of Michelle's wedding, I knew that I had been able to help her achieve. I knew that she would have an attitude of love, not fear, when coping with her life. I also knew that she would always come from a position of positive self-esteem and have the security of being unconditionally loved, that she would always believe that 'day by day, it just gets better and better'.

Later that morning the sun was shining brightly, without a cloud in the sky, and the household was buzzing with pre-wedding excitement. I suddenly became aware of Michelle standing in the doorway looking at me. She gave me a soft and gentle smile and I saw an expression of deep love in her eyes. It was as though she knew my thoughts and had shared with me the memories of her past. During that moment we shared the essence of compassion and a deep mutual understanding which I will never forget. It was as if we acknowledged each other from a 'soul' level, the other's 'knowing'.

I have a profound sense of peace in the knowledge that Michelle can cope with her world. I thank her from the bottom of my heart for the experience of being her mother. She was the instrument of my personal growth as a parent, my Karma-Kerma and gave me the opportunity to learn and experience the lessons of life.

The doctors who told me that Michelle would only be able to cope in an institutional environment were wrong. The doctor who said that Michelle would 'never amount to anything' and that 'she would need medication for the rest of her life' was wrong.

'How did the wedding go?' you ask. It was wonderful. Michelle looked the princess that she is and her husband-to-be David was her dream come true. The day went without a hitch, the sun sparkled, the birds sang and everything was just perfect.

Just as I imagined it would be!

Someone once said...
'To err is human, to forgive is divine.'

But to forgive, one must have first made a judgement!
Do we have the right to judge others?

Joane Goulding

chapter three

The central issue of self-esteem

What do parents really want for their children?

OVER THE YEARS OF TEACHING SLEEPTALK™ for Children and talking to parents about the dreams they have for their offspring, the child's basic foundation of belief or self-esteem becomes an important underlying factor. Whether it's career success, financial security, good health, a stable marriage or any other desirable asset, nothing is really possible without good self-esteem, a positive attitude and the experience and acceptance of love.

Invariably I find that the qualities of positive attitude are based on a feeling of being loved and being lovable. 'I'm OK' invariably leads to 'You're OK' as the child moves from feeling good about themselves to feeling good about the world around them. This results in a willingness to take on life's challenges without any preconceived idea of defeat or failure.

The importance of being unconditionally loved and lovable

It's important that your child really believes that you love them and that they are lovable, regardless of their achievements or failures. You may say, 'That's all very well, but I love my children already and they know how much I love them!' Undoubtedly you do and you probably tell them quite often. However, most of us don't realise that we unwittingly send mixed or negative messages to our children. Messages which can undermine confidence and spoil our child's chances of reaching their full potential and achieving real happiness.

Do you know the power of your words?

In the day to day business of being a parent, trying to establish guidelines and encourage appropriate behaviour, we often say things which, on the face of it, seem quite harmless. For instance, we may say, 'You're such a little terror!' as we grab our child for a hug. We know what we mean but a child's world is very literal and a message like that, repeated over and over, will become part of his or her reality. Such a message may be interpreted in any number of ways: 'She likes me to be a terror? Why does she like me and not like me? ... I get rewarded when I'm a terror; I got smacked yesterday when she called me a little terror but today I got hugged.' Confusion may occur, creating doubt, and a snowball effect of disharmony is created.

These negative messages can sneak into our relationships with our children so easily, becoming communication habits which are hard to break. 'You're so clumsy, you'd forget your head if it wasn't screwed on!' 'Ben is just like me — hopeless at maths!' These are all examples of innocent exclamations of parental frustration which, repeated often enough can cause enormous damage to the belief structures on which our children build their self-image and therefore their future.

Parents are not the only ones who make these comments from time to time. Our children receive negative or mixed messages from others in their world, from other primary-care givers such as crèche staff, high school teachers, relatives and even friends. School in particular is a minefield of negative suggestions. I'm sure some of these will sound familiar to many of you: 'You won't succeed, you're too lazy and you're late as usual'. At school you may have heard a teacher say, 'What a hopeless speller you are, you will never amount to anything in your life, you just can't concentrate'.

We unwittingly influence our children's future

Sometimes a frustrating home environment or particularly difficult circumstances can create special problems. When my daughter Michelle was little, before I became aware of the enormous power of the mind to create its own reality, I and others around her unwittingly compounded her sense of 'difference' and gave her very good reasons to behave badly and make no effort.

For instance, Michelle's younger sister, Teresa, would try and help Michelle with her speech by speaking for her. As you can imagine, the result was further frustration for Michelle, causing deeper resentment and contributing to her developing belief that she was inadequate. If Michelle was unable to turn on the television then Teresa or I would turn it on for her. If she was unable to open the door, we would open it for her. If she couldn't express what she wanted, we would keep guessing and offering suggestions until we got it right. It got to the stage where we were doing Michelle's living for her.

I also spent much of my time apologising to others in front of Michelle, 'I'm sorry, little Michelle can't speak very well' or 'I'm sorry, Michelle won't be able to manage that.' In hindsight it's little wonder that she made such slow progress in those years. Michelle learnt very quickly that there was so much she was incapable of. Why should she try? She was being told by her world that she was 'not OK', that she couldn't achieve, and that she was not capable. Gradually a belief structure formed which was to play a profound role in Michele's ability to cope with her world. Her self-image and self-esteem were negative; every thought and attempt at learning was based on a negative self-image. The concept of 'I'm not OK' became part of Michelle's basic thought patterns.

Michelle's attitude gradually worsened. She became physically violent and emotionally dysfunctional, angry and very unhappy. The thought pattern 'I'm not OK and neither is the world' became solidly entrenched as a truth in Michelle's subconscious mind.

Reaching individual potential

There was so much to learn before we could help Michelle. The first thing I had to learn as a parent was to forgive myself. Children do not come into the world with a '*How to* … ' manual attached. As parents we do and say what we think is right at the time. 20/20 vision is brilliant in its clarity; in hindsight we can all be experts.

About this time I was lucky enough to meet my future, but now deceased, husband Jim, a psychotherapist who would set me on the path to creating the miracle from which this process grew.

Although we embarked upon our journey of exploration to help a little girl with some really big problems, what we learned will also be of enormous value to your child. Whether he or she is gifted, has special needs or is pretty much just like the rest of us, it will be of help to you. This is a process about reaching individual potentials, whatever they may be.

Your child may not be intellectually impaired or suffer from brain damage, your child may not have an impairment that restricts their ability to talk or walk or laugh and cry, and your child may be well and happy. Does that mean they could not benefit from this extra help? Of course they can. All children, regardless of ability, attitude to life and their environment will benefit from this process. We all need to have that confidence, that deep inner belief of 'knowing'; the belief that 'I'm OK.' That mum and dad love me, even if I have been 'naughty'. It is the action of the child that parents sometimes dislike or disagree with, not the child. Can we be certain that our children know the subtle difference between them?

Perhaps if you asked yourself the question, when was the last time I told my child, my husband or perhaps my friend, that I loved them? Was it today or perhaps last week, maybe it's been some time since you expressed your thoughts. If so, consider how important it is to share these thoughts with our loved ones. Most of us enjoy that continual expression of love, regardless of age or sex, not only demonstrated by action or deed, but by expressing the words, 'I love you'.

It's important to gain an understanding of how the process of SleepTalk™ was developed and subsequently used. The underpinning knowledge, the background and contributing aspects that make this powerful process work need to be thoroughly discussed and appreciated.

You are a child of the Universe
No less than the trees and the stars,
You have the right to be here
And whether or not it is clear to you,
No doubt the Universe is
Unfolding as it should.
Therefore be at peace with God,
Whatever you conceive
Him to be.

From Desiderata

chapter four
What happens to thoughts when we sleep

The modern subconscious

THERE IS AN AREA OR ASPECT OF THE MIND we need to be aware of before we discuss the actual SleepTalk™ process. It's called the modern subconscious. This is a part of the mind which stores the memories of one waking period, from when you first awaken until you next go to sleep. The modern subconscious has several interesting characteristics. One of them is that it has limited memory-capacity, which is one of the reasons why, when someone works too hard or too long, they get confused, have difficulty concentrating and become very tired. When the modern subconscious has reached its capacity for memory, unlike the subconscious, everything which has occurred throughout the waking time is still open to review and change. Unlike the subconscious, its memories have not yet become belief or 'fact' within the subconscious.

When we sleep, we go through cycles called brain wave frequencies. When rapid eye movement REM occurs during the sleep state, it means that we are dreaming; sifting through memory in the modern subconscious; deciding how we feel about what has happened throughout the day so we can process those thoughts, feelings and reactions, and allow them to find their way into the subconscious mind. If we don't get it all done then, we come back and do some more later, until we have worked through all the information gathered in that day according to how we feel about it, because ultimately, we are feeling creatures. We don't file it away by date, and we don't file it under, 'I saw an elephant today'. What becomes the memory is 'how big the elephant was' and what feelings were experienced. Was it exciting or was it scary?

As we sleep through the night some of the day's occurrences that have been stored in our modern subconscious are then processed as dreams. Sometimes we can't decide how we feel about something so we have another little area tucked away called the 'too hard basket'. I'm sure that's not the correct technical term but for this discussion its fine. As we go through the different cycles of sleep during the night, which we will discuss in the next chapter, we eventually deal with most of the memories from that particular day. The memories that we haven't been able to deal with are placed in the 'too-hard basket' which we visit repeatedly. If we have now gathered enough information to deal with some of these issues, which we couldn't understand or reconcile before, we will deal with them; if not, they stay there.

So each day we gather more information to see if we can now deal with issues in that 'too hard basket'. If we can't deal with them, we are likely to get repetitive dreams or nightmares. Notice that it usually happens in the early hours of the morning, not at the commencement of sleep. Initially we are dealing with information that is easy to cope with. Then we get to the 'too hard basket'. So if children are having bad dreams or nightmares, they have something in the 'too hard basket' that they can't reconcile. When something enters the subconscious mind it becomes belief and it's very hard to change it. However, the modern subconscious has a short-term memory which can change. When something occurs throughout the day you continually add new information to the previously accepted knowledge, allowing you to understand it a little better. You may even change your opinion about issues. In other words, memories compound.

A few days later something happens that seems to be in conflict with that memory — now an accepted belief within the subconscious mind — and you are quite likely to argue and say, 'Hey, that's not how I understood it'. The belief is now harder to change. For example, let's say that you are in the kitchen preparing the meal. You pick up the mixer and its cord gets caught around a litre of milk and falls onto the floor. As you try and catch it you knock all the eggs over. You turn around to get the tea towel and of course it's sitting on the flour bag — and you now have cake mix on the floor! You don't feel really terrific about this; and it occurred because you weren't concentrating very well, or because there was something on your mind.

You're in a hurry to clean it up and as you begin, two little feet in gumboots walk right through the middle of the mess, then slip over and sit in it. In your frustration you might shout out, 'Didn't I tell you not to bother me when I'm cooking, get out of here — you're always in the way, you're such a pest. Don't worry me with unimportant things right now'.

You really didn't mean what you said but you said it. We have all said things like that. We all say in a moment of frustration or distraction something we don't mean. The problem is, regardless of the truth, the thought occurring in your child's young mind might be, 'I'm mum's biggest problem, I'm not important, I'm in the way'. Thoughts the child may accept as a belief.

At the time you were upset and didn't mean what you said. But a child in that situation sees your distress and their limited perception may mistakenly take on board the belief that they were the reason for you feeling upset. The child may become very emotional, feeling rejected and confused. That misunderstanding or belief is all primed and ready — whether true or not — to journey into the subconscious mind during sleep that night.

The conscious mind is unable at that moment to evaluate the thought processes. So what do we do about it? If we let the child go to sleep with the belief, 'I'm mum's biggest problem', every time mum gets upset about something that belief may be reinforced. The child may take responsibility for situations, become guilty, become very upset and the belief, 'I'm mum's biggest problem' may become part of that child's belief structure.

Dealing with issues before sleep

So what do we do if this situation occurs? How do we deal with issues correctly? If possible, deal with the issue before sleep, sit down on the side of the bed and perhaps say to them, 'Darling, when you were in the kitchen before and I yelled at you, remember the mess on the floor and how upset I was? Well, I'm like you, sometimes when I'm upset I say things I don't mean, and I really didn't mean what I said. You're not my biggest problem, you're my greatest joy. I don't know what I would do without you. I love you.'

We present an alternative explanation *and* the solution to their dilemma straight away. When they go to sleep the explanation and the memory of distress will be accepted as a complete unit, as an already resolved issue, not a problem. In fact, a deeper understanding of the situation may occur. They may think, 'Hey, mum loves me, everyone gets upset sometimes. We all say things we don't really mean. It's OK though, they love me.'

It is so important to deal with a mistake, and the worse the mistake, the more reason to fix it. If you say something and realise that you shouldn't have, if possible fix it before you go to sleep.

What happens if you get impatient, upset or hurt with your partner? The same situation will occur. Don't ever let them go to sleep with unresolved issues, talk it through, because the same process happens to you. Communication is so important — things are so easily misunderstood and so easily taken out of context. Try not to allow the issues to become a concrete belief in the other person's subconscious belief system. Deal with it, even though it can be difficult and sometimes embarrassing.

Communicate with your child and say, 'I made a mistake, I didn't mean it, I do love you, it was your behaviour that annoyed me not you, I didn't mean those things I said today'. As a result your child may not feel quite so guilty when they do the same thing or say something that they didn't mean. They may also come back to you and say, 'Hey, I'm sorry, I didn't mean it'. That's a rather lovely quality to give to your child isn't it, the courage, the confidence, the self-esteem and the security to be able to say those things.

The younger the child, the more open they are to suggestions and to changes to their belief structure. Because the mind is a protective filter that develops as we grow, its purpose is to protect us. When we are very young everyone is an authority over us — which is why SleepTalk™ is so vital a tool for parents. The communication factor is vital to understand because of the developing conscious critical factor within children. This is why the SleepTalk™ process works best between the ages of approximately two years of age through to puberty.

As our children grow, memories keep compounding as circumstances keep occurring. Unfortunately they are not all going to be good and positive; because we cannot be with our children all the time, we cannot protect them all the time. There are other carers in their lives. So there comes a time, either from mum or dad or another primary carer, when a cross word is said and suddenly the child is jolted out of its comfortable cocoon of thought. Those first negative or cross words are accepted without conscious, critical analysis into the subconscious mind. They will also awaken the development of the ability of the mind to analyse. That protective mechanism sits over everything. As we go through life and get bolder and older and the experiences become more traumatic and more powerful, our mind protects us more and more. Unfortunately, it protects us blindly according to the beliefs that are lodged in the deep subconscious of our mind. It protects us regardless because the mind is impersonal. It will protect us from anything that doesn't fit alongside our basic belief structure, whether true or false.

SleepTalk™ has the ability to correct that situation. It is so simple, it is so powerful. We use exactly the same processes to re-educate the memory and correct the negative beliefs. The same process that allowed the subconscious mind to believe, 'I'm not OK, I'm not secure, I'm not confident'.

SleepTalk™ for Children corrects negative beliefs. We don't always remember consciously where initial thoughts or fears originate from. All we have are accepted beliefs of truth, both positive and negative. So let us investigate exactly what is meant by brain wave frequencies and what relevance they have to SleepTalk™.

chapter five

Brain wave frequency and your child

IN THE EARLY 1950S WHILE RESEARCHING THE PHENOMENON we call sleep, Eugene Aserinsky, a graduate student working under the direction of Professor of Physiology Nathaniel Kleitmen at the University of Chicago, discovered that while sleeping a person experiences rapid eye movement, sometimes called REM for short. The finding proved that the brain is active during sleep and pointed sleep research in a new direction.

Consciousness, including sleep, has in fact many different levels, but to keep it simple we will describe only a few of them. The hertz frequencies are approximate.

Level of Consciousness	Hertz Frequency	Consciousness State
Beta	14 – 40	Waking State
Alpha – REM	7 – 14	Relaxed State – Daydreaming
Theta – REM	3.5 – 7	Deep Relaxation – Dreams
Delta – Non-REM	0.25 – 3.5	Very Deep Sleep –Recovery

As can be seen from the above table there are two rapid eye movement (REM) levels. The first is Alpha, with a brain wave frequency of approximately 7 to 14 hertz per second. The second is Theta, at approximately 3.5 to 7 hertz per second. The one Non-REM level is called Delta, at approximately 0.25 to 3.5 hertz per second.

The most important fact to remember is that for the SleepTalk™ process to work we need to make sure that the child is in a REM level of consciousness. It is during the REM level of sleep that new, positive suggestions can be accepted, without the critical conscious mind rejecting them. The ideal level seems to be between Alpha and Theta; the optimum is when both frequencies are simultaneously active and present in high amplitudes (activity). It is therefore important that a routine procedure be established to access the correct brain wave frequency for SleepTalk™ to work, while at the same time not awakening the child. It took us over two years to perfect the process but our persistence paid off.

The thought process operating within the subconscious mind in regard to mentally and physically impaired individuals is no different to that which operates in so called 'normal' children.

If a thought, emotion or image has been experienced, accepted and eventually lodged within the subconscious memory it becomes reality, part of the belief system of that individual. Like the hard drive of a computer, once accepted into the memory bank of the subconscious mind the memory expresses itself through consciousness when activated. Because Michelle had brain damage she needed the visual aspect to stimulate recall of a memory. For example, a photograph would activate the recorded thought, allowing the memory a path back to conciousness.

The pathway of thought

One day while travelling with Michelle, she started to say something while pointing excitedly out of the car window to an empty paddock. We couldn't understand what she was saying or indeed what she meant. It wasn't until later that evening we discovered that, 'Ooh, ook, ircus' represented the memory of a circus which we had visited the previous year. Michelle's memory of the circus had been activated by seeing an empty paddock, and she was able to recall the memory of a circus after a whole year. In other words if a suggestion, emotion, thought, feeling or reaction, whether true or imagined, fact or fiction, is received and accepted by the subconscious mind then it is retrievable. Again, similar to a computer, what goes in to the memory can be retrieved.

The difference between the human mind and a computer memory is that the subconscious mind will record all the thoughts, feelings and reactions that are being experienced by the individual at that time. The computer only accepts the input of information given, which is an important point to remember if you are studying. If you study while you are anxious or upset, when it's time to retrieve that knowledge or memory, the chances are you will also retrieve the negative emotions or thoughts that you were experiencing at that time. Further, the mind may resist the retrieval of these memories as a defence against experiencing a replay of linked negative feelings. Well to consider playing soft and relaxing music while studying.

With Michelle we had the additional difficulty of knowing that children with brain damage or impaired perception sometimes process suggestions or information differently to that which was given. Their translation or interpretation of the message becomes distorted, and in many cases what was recorded within the subconscious mind becomes a different image or suggestion to that which was accepted initially.

Michelle had the belief that she was not 'OK' and that her world was not a happy one. This negative belief was compounded by the translation distortion and by the fact that she lacked the ability to concentrate or indeed converse and understand fully what was being said to her. But that was on a conscious level only, because subconsciously she was no different. If we could access her subconscious mind directly, bypassing the conscious mind without the interference of the conscious critical 'I'm not OK' thought and belief, surely we could create a confident 'I'm OK' belief structure to replace the accepted negative one.

The only time that it was possible to access Michelle's subconscious mind was while she was asleep. Her level of concentration was extremely short, so suggestions during waking hours were unrealistic. In addition, her anger and aggression interfered with co-operating with directions or suggestions.

Acceptance of suggestion without critical analysis

When sleep takes over at the end of the day the brain wave frequency changes and fluctuates between a number of different frequencies. These brain wave frequencies, as we explained earlier, are called Beta, Alpha, Theta and Delta and can be measured on an electroencephalograph (EEG) machine. The EEG works like an amplifier with wires connected to electrodes, which are placed on the scalp. The machine records and graphs the electrical activities inside the brain which, like a broadcasting and receiving transmitter, runs on electricity, similar to a radio station which operates on different frequencies or bands. The brain's frequencies range from 0.25 up to as high as 35 – 40 and are divided into four levels or channels, and like a radio, only one channel is active at any given time.

The classification relies on the frequency of the waves rather than their strength. The unit of frequency is called the hertz, named after Heinrich Hertz, who discovered the electrical signal in 1929. Believing this signal to be the basic brain wave pattern, and certainly the strongest, he named it 'Alpha' — sometimes called the relaxation, or super conscious level, of mind. By doubling the Alpha range Hertz classified Beta, identified by waking consciousness, alertness or mental activity; by halving Alpha he arrived at Theta, identified by deep states of relaxation, memory recall and nightmares. Delta is the last stage (half the Hertz frequency of Theta), and is identified by deep coma or deep sleep.

At this level of brain wave frequency you are completely unaware of your physical body. It is the deepest level of consciousness, allowing the physical body to recover (sometimes called the 'Airsdale' state). If suddenly awoken from this level, disorientation and irritability may be experienced. The usual cycle of time for a healthy adult whilst asleep would be approximately 90 minutes, with only a short span of time in Delta.

Beta is the brain wave frequency that we experience whilst awake and engaging in activity. Alpha is experienced when we daydream or relax and is also the level that we drift into when going to sleep. Theta is the deeper level of sleep between Alpha and Delta. Delta is the deepest level where the body heals, grows, recovers from illness or when in a coma. Newborn babies are in the lower levels of brain wave frequency during the first few months of life; as they grow and become less needful of sleep their brain wave frequencies remain less in the Delta level than when an infant.

The Top Hat theory

Whilst asleep the conscious mind rests and dreams but the subconscious mind never loses awareness, even when at the lowest level of Delta. It is now a proven fact that a person in a coma can hear what is being said to them, that a person under anaesthetic can return to full awareness and repeat what has been said during the operation.

While Michelle slept we were able to suggest positive messages directly into her subconscious mind (the computer), we could bypass the negative conscious 'I'm not OK' belief which would cause critical rejection. Positive suggestions introduced would become both a reality lodged deeply into the subconscious mind and an accepted fact or belief for Michelle. If repeated regularly, the power of positive suggestions would eventually become stronger than the foothold of the negative ones. With this process the previous auto-suggestions or beliefs of truth would not be able to interfere with Michelle's acceptance of the positive suggestions.

SleepTalk™ suggestions bypass the conscious critical analysis of the conscious mind — what we call the 'Top Hat'. As a consequence, those suggestions are accepted without the negative interference from any previous thoughts, feelings or reactions. The new positive thoughts or beliefs accepted into the subconscious mind eventually find their own access or pathway through to consciousness. It was Michelle's conscious mind that had been damaged, not her subconscious.

The key to SleepTalk™ is the acceptance of suggestion without critical analyses. We hypothesised … if specific suggestions were presented and accepted by Michelle's subconscious mind without rejection or distortion from the conscious mind they would become fact. By presenting information, suggestions or facts into the memory banks of Michelle's subconscious mind then we knew it would be possible for them to be retrieved into conscious thought.

In October 2003 *The Age* newspaper (Melbourne, Australia) reported that researchers at Victoria University found that beeping smoke alarms may not wake young children in the event of a fire; that 50% of the time young children will sleep through a piercing beep, but a recording of a parent's voice calling the child is guaranteed to wake them. The researchers even found that a recording of an actor shouting, 'Wake up, wake up, there is a fire' is better than 90% effective.

Dorothy Bruck, the leader of the Victoria University team, conducted some of her research on her own children. She commented that, 'We still do not know much about sleep. The brains of young children are still developing and they sleep much more deeply than mature adults. Yet, however deep their sleep, they are always aware of and respond to a parent's voice. It appears that the human brain, even in sleep, constantly monitors the frequency range of a human voice and even adults respond more readily to the sound of their name than to a beep'.

Why SleepTalk™ works

Mortimer Mishkin and Tim Appenzeller (1987) conducted an inquiry into the roots of human amnesia, which showed how deep structures in the brain may interact with perceptual pathways in outer brain layers to transform sensory stimuli into memories. At the conclusion of their studies they were still unsure of the activity in the human brain regarding memory. My late husband and I didn't have the knowledge of a surgeon or a psychologist, so for us it was easier to keep things simple. Maybe that is why this process worked, because we didn't know it supposedly couldn't!

Michelle could not concentrate and had difficulty co-operating with us. So even trying to access her subconscious mind whilst in a waking conscious state with the normal process of suggestion was not possible. The only option was to work with her whilst she was asleep. If the conscious mind or the negative conscious critical aspect remained asleep and dreaming in the Alpha level she would not be able to reject suggestions directed to the subconscious mind. If we were able to do all of this without the negative 'I'm not OK' belief rejecting our suggestions and comments, those positive suggestions would eventually become accepted thoughts/beliefs of the subconscious mind.

Could such a simple process, taking only a few moments to complete, have such a dramatic result? If, without her awakening or rejecting our suggestions, we were able to access Michelle's sub-conscious memory banks, telling her she was unconditionally loved, that she was OK, that she could talk and walk and that she was a happy child whose mum and family loved her ... wouldn't that be a miracle? We thought so.

Receiving transmitter — the mind's antenna

The SleepTalk™ for Children step-by-step explanation of why the 'Top Hat' procedure works is detailed. Whilst asleep the conscious mind rests but the subconscious mind retains a level of awareness. Some call it the Reticular Activating System (RAS); it's as though the subconscious mind has a receiving antenna all of its own which at some level is always aware.

The researchers at Victoria University tried to determine what tells us to wake up when deeply asleep. What alerts us to awaken when our children cry out or a car back-fires? It's the 'antenna' of our subconscious mind, and it's always 'tuned' in. We simply named or described the phenomena as the 'mind's antenna.' Radios need an antenna to receive information and the mind is the same. (See diagram 1.)

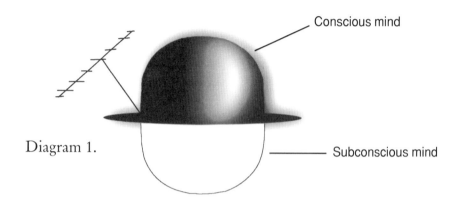

Diagram 1.

Conscious mind

Subconscious mind

For example, when your baby cries out in the night you wake, even if your baby is two doors away, yet you may remain asleep when a car backfires as it passes the house. It's the 'antenna' of the subconscious mind which determines the difference.

As part of the SleepTalk™ process, we direct our child's conscious mind, the 'Top Hat', to stay asleep by communicating with the subconscious mind via the 'antenna'. For SleepTalk™ to be effective it's imperative to talk to the subconscious 'antenna' to engage the correct brain wave frequency. In other words, take off the 'Top Hat' (the conscious mind) and tell it to continue sleeping, allowing direct access to the subconscious mind. (See diagram 2.)

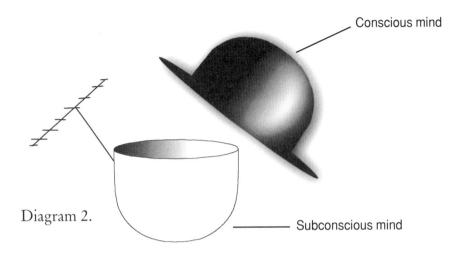

Conscious mind

Diagram 2.

Subconscious mind

The SleepTalk™ process enables you to talk directly to the subconscious mind of your child without interference from the conscious mind. The conscious mind may be influenced by negative beliefs previously accepted as fact by the subconscious mind. (See diagram 3.)

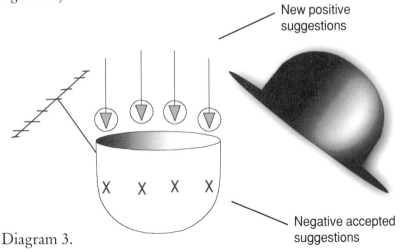

New positive suggestions

Negative accepted suggestions

Diagram 3.

At this particular point *everything* you say to your child is critical, so please make sure all external noises or conversations, e.g. the TV or people talking, are eliminated. The phrases or suggestions that we present as part of the 'Foundation' process have been researched and proven over 30 years to be most beneficial and effective, reinforcing the belief of unconditional love and self-esteem.

When presented to the subconscious mind in this specific manner, these positive phrases will be accepted, without consideration and hence possible rejection. They sit next to the negative beliefs in the subconscious mind of your child. (See Diagram 4.)

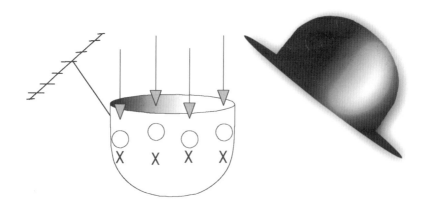

Diagram 4.

To complete the process you say, 'Deep asleep – deep asleep'. The suggestions will direct the conscious mind, the 'Top Hat', to a deeper brain wave frequency of sleep. In other words, put back the 'Top Hat' (See Diagram 5.)

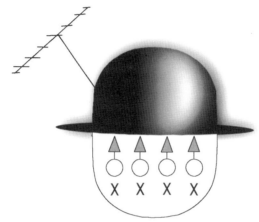

Diagram 5.

Over time the positive phrases given during SleepTalk™ will dominate or dilute the energy of any negative beliefs. The positive suggestions will be accepted within the deep subconscious mind of your child and become fact. Positive suggestions of self-image, confidence and a belief that their world is happy will dominate. This is the core of this powerful process of positive parenting.

If you always do what you've always done,
you will always get what you've always got.
Anon

chapter six
SleepTalk™ — the underpinning knowledge

WE HAVE DISCUSSED THE 'TOP HAT' PROCESS and explained the importance of suggestions given to our children. We now need to look at the 'Foundation' process, a combination of the 'Top Hat' process and the basic SleepTalk™ method. The basic suggestions are only spoken when the appropriate brain wave frequency is achieved — in other words, the 'Top Hat' process has been instigated. This allows the conscious mind to remain asleep whilst the subconscious mind remains alert and receptive. The procedure not only bypasses conscious critical analysis, which may lead to rejection or misinterpretation, but also ensures that the child is at the appropriate and correct level of brain wave frequency, a major problem with other sleep-learning methods.

SleepTalk™ allows parents to become part of the healing, learning and educational progress of their child. It allows a safe medium for parents to communicate, express and show their love without fear of possible rejection.

Many people have difficulty in expressing their love, conversely some have difficulty in accepting it. This process allows for a gentle, non-intrusive, ethical and personal exchange of that primary emotion — without fear of rejection — that is so essential to all.

Basic ground rules before commencing SleepTalk™

Basic rules to be observed with SleepTalk™ include:

» SleepTalk™ works more quickly and efficiently if there is total involvement from both parents and caregivers.

» When giving suggestions during the SleepTalk™ process never use persuasion, as this will cause critical analysis and awaken the child.

» Do not use 'Specific Suggestions' or work with the 'Primary' area of need until you have observed basic 'Feedback' which we will discuss in a later chapter.

» If possible, repeat the SleepTalk™ process every night and during the day in general conversation as this helps eliminate confusion in the child's mind.

It is important that both parents conduct the SleepTalk™ process. The child gains their basic self-image from both parents and in the case of a single or divorced parent, the importance of including both 'mummy and daddy' in the suggestions must be stressed. This may be a very difficult, painful and sensitive area for some single-parent families. If I discuss this with you from an intellectual aspect rather than an emotional perspective it may assist you to fully understand and appreciate that single parents must allow the child the right to love the other parent.

The child may sometimes adopt the belief that it is not acceptable, or disloyal, to love 'the other parent', and this may cause the child to feel guilty about loving the other parent. Do not put your child in the position of having to choose.

Resentment

It is necessary at this stage to mention resentment. Any areas of resentment, or fear, need to be addressed between parents; the need is even greater in the case of single-parent families.

The following points may assist you.

» Resentment causes great unhappiness for family members.

» As a single parent you may feel you have the right to feel resentful about specific situations, especially towards the other party in a stressed relationship. Unfortunately, this only serves to create unhappiness in the person who is allowing the negative emotions of resentment to interfere with their life.

» If your child doesn't feel comfortable allowing the parent who has primary custody to know they love the other parent as well, it can cause guilt, resentment and fear. Remember, the subconscious self-image of your child comes from both parents.

» It is important to remember that parents' emotional displays reflect back to children. Children don't have the same ability as adults to reject negative emotions and suggestions. Conscious suggestions to an adult are dealt with critically and analytically. In a child's mind, this critical analysis is less effective. Therefore most suggestions, especially if given by someone in authority over your child's mind automatically becomes 'auto-suggestion', lodged deep in the sub-conscious mind. Emotional disharmony may result, staying with the child for many years.

General background guidelines

When we were designing the SleepTalk™ process it was necessary to develop a list of competencies that would assist us to successfully achieve the outcomes we were working towards. A number of issues had to be discussed:

» Identify the major issues or concerns.

» Formulate a procedure that would eradicate or address the issues, being mindful of the potential ramifications of suggestion.

» Develop a methodology for parents who would be conducting the SleepTalk™ process; detail the suggestions to be used and the reasons why.

» The suggestions must not use persuasion.

» Be aware of the 'down line' ramifications of the suggestions. For example, 'You will enjoy school … you won't be afraid of your teacher' is not an acceptable suggestion. Situations may arise in the future where fear is an appropriate reaction to a teacher; conversely, this suggestion may initiate an association of 'fear' with learning. In addition, persuasion has been used.

» Suggestions, especially the basic 'Foundation' ones, must be repeated during the waking hours: reinforcement enables your child to correctly associate the suggestion to an everyday event.

» The words or suggestions used must be appropriate to the child's level of perception and logic.

It is important to remember that the 'Foundation' suggestions are just as significant in the waking state as they are in the sleep state. An added bonus of this process is to bring to your attention the power that suggestions have. From this moment on always be mindful of correct communication with members of your family.

In the case of Michelle, SleepTalk™ started with the full understanding and co-operation of her stepfather, my late husband Jim. Over a period of two years the new, positive and happy self-image suggestions were accepted by Michelle. Gradually she became less anxious and aggressive, more affectionate, friendly and confident.

The process was amended from time to time in order to focus on specific areas of need such as speech, co-ordination of movement and social behaviour. During this time her progress was monitored by the daycare centre she attended. Her anger and aggression were gradually reducing and a decision not to use sedative medication was made.

Acceptance of positive suggestions

We discovered that the positive self-image suggestions had to be fully accepted by the subconscious mind before we could attempt to correct any specific areas of need. As with any new structure, the foundation groundwork must be established before initiating any modifications.

When the time came to work on the 'Primary Area' of need for Michelle, emphasis was given to the co-ordination of movement of limbs (walking and swimming), survival skills including speech, reading and writing and, most importantly, socially acceptable behaviour. The program was amended each time positive feedback indicated acceptance of a specific suggestion. The suggestions were also changed to reflect the progressive, deeper understanding and acceptance of those suggestions.

It took many years of patience for the full process to be implemented but the results were rewarding. Because of my integral involvement in the SleepTalk™ process I was able to communicate and express love to Michelle, without having to deal with continued rejection and aggression. The unexpected reward of this process was the improvement of the personal relationship between Michelle and myself.

Michelle is only one of hundreds of children who have since been helped with this method. Some of their case histories are included later. However, it's important to remember that the SleepTalk™ process works with all children.

Carefully worded statements

The 'Foundation' process consists of carefully worded statements which are lovingly delivered to your child each night just after they have fallen asleep. We call it the 'Foundation' process because it is these suggestions and statements which will give your child a solid foundation of self-esteem. We reinforce, or establish, a deeply held accepted belief that they are both unconditionally loved and lovable. This belief not only gives your child positive self-esteem and a wonderful opportunity to know they can achieve and reach their goals in life, but also helps them greatly with any habitual behaviours or difficulties. When you have mastered the 'Foundation' process and noticed sufficient feedback, indicating that the process' suggestions have been accepted by your child's subconscious mind (which we discuss later in much more detail), additional suggestions to tackle specific issues relevant to your child can be added.

I have mentioned previously that the SleepTalk™ process is primarily effective for children from about two years of age to puberty — normally 10–12 years depending on individual maturity. This is because, as children develop, they gain the ability to make decisions based on their accepted belief structure. As they develop their beliefs, so do they develop their ability for conscious critical analysis. As your child enters adolescence, and conscious critical analysis strengthens, the effectiveness of the process diminishes. If your child is coping with an intellectual, emotional and/or behavioural impairment, the changes may take longer, but the positive side to this is that the process continues to be effective for much longer.

Back to the basic process. After about one or two weeks of using the SleepTalk™ 'Foundation' process (covered in the next chapter), you will be able to observe subtle and gradual changes in your child's behaviour. We call this 'feedback'. Positive changes may be very subtle, or quite dramatic and therefore easily identified. Feedback normally occurs between seven and ten days after you have commenced, but can often be noticed earlier. Conversely it has even taken up to six weeks to become evident. However, if you stop SleepTalk™ too early, you may find that the second time around it will take longer for feedback to occur and in many cases it is not so easily identifiable. More importantly, the gains you have made will be lost because not enough reinforcement was given. If this occurs it's possible that the negative or inappropriate behaviour or attitudes will return to pre-SleepTalk™ times. So once you start this process, it is most important that you continue — especially when there are signs of improvement. So let's now discuss what is meant by 'Feedback'.

Signs of positive feedback

Feedback signs indicate change is taking place and that the 'Foundation' process is working as planned. Examples will be covered in much greater detail in a later chapter, but the different areas that can be addressed include:

Social — examples of feedback. There may be an improvement in speech, movement, co-ordination, and general awareness. There can be a better comprehension of what is being said and what is going on, improved memory and more enjoyable play with other children. Your child may be less influenced by peer pressure, have the confidence to say 'No' and show an improvement in general health.

Mood state and self-esteem — examples of feedback. Your child might feel happier on awakening, feel more energetic and self-confident. You may notice: a change in their self-esteem, improved optimism, and generally less shy, anxious or aggressive behaviour. Specific conditions such as bed-wetting, hypertension, asthma or nail bitting may all improve. Your child may be less attention seeking, have improved concentration and sleep better at night.

Family and communications — examples of feedback. Within the family unit your child may well be more co-operative, responsive and open to meaningful communication. There may be less conflict with siblings, better focus on homework and a more open expression of love and care to all around. There could be improved eating habits and involvement with the family. In short, a happier child.

Attitude to school — examples of feedback. School life, both academically and socially, could also show signs of improvement, and study may become a more enjoyable task. There may be less anxiety about doing well, which usually results in better performance.

Over the years it was my great pleasure to work with parents and I recorded some of the workshop conversations. Included in later chapters and throughout this book are excerpts from those recorded interviews. They will give you a clear insight regarding the possible feedback that occurs when you start to use this great process. Remember, the 'Foundation' process is relevant for all children regardless of their individual needs.

Basic security

The 'Foundation' process gives your child a basic security and a feeling of wellbeing. Their increasingly positive self-image and confidence, how they feel about their place in the world will be of enormous value to them throughout their lives. Children have to walk their own pathway and the best that we can do as parents is to give them the skills, confidence and self-esteem needed to deal with life's inevitable difficulties, challenges and negatives. Children need to be able to deal with sibling rivalry, peer group pressures and situations threatening to their self-esteem.

Actively protecting your child

You, as a loving guardian, now have the opportunity of actively protecting your child against the thieves of self-esteem. SleepTalk™ will enable your child to utilise their full potential. As a parent, please be assured that the SleepTalk™ process you are about to commence will empower you to assist your child to utilise that potential. Give them their right to succeed and enjoy life.

chapter seven
SleepTalk™ — Basic 'Foundation' Process

Now that we have discussed the 'Top Hat' process in theory it's time to really gain an understanding of the complete process. This chapter will discuss the 'Foundation' process in detail and give you a very clear and concise description of how to conduct SleepTalk™ for Children.

The 'Foundation' process is a group of carefully worded statements which are lovingly delivered by you to your child each night just after they have fallen asleep. We call it the 'Foundation' process because it is these statements which will give your child a solid foundation of self-esteem by reinforcing or establishing a deeply held belief that they are both unconditionally loved and lovable and that their world is a happy place. This belief not only gives your child a wonderful opportunity to reach their full goals in life, but also assists with any distress, inappropriate behaviours or difficulties. After you have mastered the 'Foundation' process and have noticed sufficient feedback you may wish to add some 'Support' suggestions to address specific issues, e.g. bed-wetting or nail-biting.

So let's get started. Make sure that your child has been asleep for at least 30–45 minutes. Allow sufficient light into the bedroom to allow you to see any movement that might take place and be able to read the script. Walk — do not creep into the child's bedroom. Creeping may activate the child's curiosity and wake them.

It doesn't matter if other children are in the room — just repeat the procedure with each child separately, lowering your voice to minimise any disturbance to other children. If your child is a heavy sleeper, the process may take a little longer to activate than a child who is a light sleeper. Remember, the brain wave frequency fluctuates throughout the night.

Engage the correct brain wave frequency

If your child is facing you, gently stroke their forehead. If facing away from you, gently stroke from the crown of the head to the back of the neck, saying in a soft, gentle, slow voice, 'Stay asleep, stay asleep'. Do not speak at normal pace. Slow your speech down, but do not whisper, as it may activate awareness.

Repeat the stroking and the words, 'Stay asleep — stay asleep' until you see a movement, any movement. This could be a twitch of the limbs, a yawn, opening of the eyes or licking of the lips. The child may even sit up. Do not be concerned if the child talks to you or appears to awaken, just continue. They are still in the Alpha level of awareness and may not even remember the events the next day.

No suggestions should be given until this movement takes place.

Despite any movement, the child will probably still appear to be asleep. However, do not be misled into thinking they cannot hear you. All mind units are concentrating on your voice. Any communication with your child must now be carefully and very correctly phrased. Make sure there is no background noise.

Immediately you become aware of movement, **stop touching** — you have reached the correct brain wave frequency for SleepTalk™ to become effective. If you continue to touch, the awareness of the conscious mind will return to a brain wave frequency where

SleepTalk™ will not be accepted. Remember, you are speaking to the subconscious area of your child's mind, an area that doesn't possess any facility for conscious, critical, logical thinking.

When you speak, speak slowly and quietly. **Do not whisper.** Whispering may awaken the child. Remember not to alter in any way the following suggestions or process — they have been carefully crafted to be effective and non-intrusive.

The 'Foundation' process consists of a few statements. Say them slowly, with feeling and without stopping. Mean them from the bottom of your heart. Although the words and statements may seem strange to you, they will not be so to your child. Repeat the statement at least three to four times, **talking slowly without whispering**:

'Mummy loves you — Daddy loves you — We all love you — You are lovable — Today is a happy day.'

On completion of the process, return your child to natural sleep by repeating the words:

'Deep asleep ... Deep asleep ... Happy dreams ... Waking up bright and happy. Mummy loves you ... Daddy loves you ... We all love you ... You are lovable ... Every day in every way it gets better and better.'

Repeat the 'Foundation' process every evening

Ensure that you repeat the 'Foundation' process each evening for at least 3–4 weeks. When feedback begins to occur, then and only then, introduce the 'Support' suggestions which we will discuss in a later chapter. Reinforcing the basic 'Foundation' process with additional 'Support' suggestions becomes most beneficial. Many parents continue SleepTalk™ through to puberty and sometimes beyond.

If you are going out for the evening, then make sure you spend a couple of moments upon return. Although it may take a little longer for your child to respond to your touch, it will happen. Whenever possible, alternate each evening, mum or dad taking it in turns. Remember, your child gains self-esteem from both parents. When a parent or parents are absent just alternate whenever possible with the primary carers of your child.

If it is not possible to conduct SleepTalk™ within the first three quarters of an hour of your child going to bed, don't be concerned. All that will happen is that it may take longer for your child to respond to your stroking. If during the process you think your child has woken, return them to sleep by repeating the words:

'Deep asleep ... Deep asleep ... Happy dreams ... Waking up bright and happy ... Mummy loves you ... Daddy loves you ... We all love you ... You are lovable ... Today is a happy day.'

All you need to do is repeat the statement, regardless of the response. If your child does not fall back to sleep, simply tell them that you love them, say 'happy dreams' and leave the room. Sometimes very anxious children may initially have difficulty in accepting the suggestions of sleep. Do not be concerned. It's only the degree of anxiety that they are trying to deal with. Just persevere each night and you will gradually discover that the level of distress or suspicion will reduce to the point where you can proceed with the process. If in any doubt contact me personally via the web site and I will guide you through the process.

What you may notice during the process

So let's just revise what we have discussed. If your child wakes during SleepTalk™ don't be concerned, just continue by quietly saying:

'Mummy loves you ... daddy loves you ...We all love you ... Deep asleep ... Deep asleep.'

Transference to the correct brain wave frequency can be assumed with movement of any part of the body. Licking of the lips, trying to push your hand away, snuggle down under the sheets or just turning over can indicate that transference has occurred. They might even nod their head in agreement, or sit up silently with eyes open or closed, the whites of their eyes showing and to all intents and purposes be wide awake. They may even get out of bed and sleepwalk. If this happens, just continue to say 'stay asleep'. They might say, 'OK', or 'go away' or 'yes', nod their heads, or just generally agree with you.

Occasionally throughout the process, the child may talk with you but have no recollection of the conversation the following day. The child may become agitated and try to push you away while at the same time appearing to be asleep. This can occur especially if the relationships and communications within the home are distressed, angry or anxious.

Dealing with confusion and abreaction

Before the positive suggestions are accepted within the subconcious mind, confusion and abreaction may occur. The positive suggestions need to gain strength to override the negative beliefs which have previously dominated and determined the self-image. The positive suggestions given may cause great confusion within the mind if negativity or anxiety is predominant. Sometimes parents have commented that the SleepTalk™ feedback was initially great, but then aggressive and angry behaviour increased, they became worried that the SleepTalk™ was inappropriate and stopped. My advice has always been to continue the SleepTalk™ because the positive suggestions will very quickly override the negative.

When anyone moves out of their comfort zone it can cause confusion and distress. For example, an anxious person may have difficulty relaxing because it feels strange and uncomfortable. Children who are particularly anxious or have difficulty sleeping may require many attempts to gain access to the correct brain wave frequency without completely awakening. If your child is young enough, attempt the SleepTalk™ process during their day-time sleep. This process is safe and non-intrusive and will work eventually if you persevere each night. Whatever occurs just continue — it's safe.

A few examples of comments children might make whilst you conduct SleepTalk™:

» 'No, you don't', which may be coupled with the arm waving you away.
» 'Yes, I know', or they may just generally agree with you.
» 'Go away'.
» 'Yes, I am clever'.

» 'I am loveable'.

» They might even say 'Yes, and I love you'.

Try not to miss a night during this 'Foundation' process. If appropriate, alternate the primary carers (partner, grandparents, etc.) who are implementing SleepTalk™. If you can conduct the process every evening you will gradually use the SleepTalk™ process without having to read from your notes and without being self-conscious. Always remember — no harm can come from SleepTalk™. It is a non-intrusive and natural process and takes only a short time to complete each session.

Feedback — Is the process working?

'Feedback' basically means that in some way or other you notice change in your child's day to day behaviour. Changes may be very subtle, or quite dramatic and therefore easily identified. 'Feedback' normally occurs between seven and ten days, but can often be noticed earlier and has even taken up to six weeks to become evident. However, if you stop the SleepTalk™ process too early, you may find that the second time around it will take longer for 'feedback' to occur and in many cases, it is not so easily identifiable.

More importantly, the gains you have made will be lost and the behaviour or attitude of your child will return to what is normal for them. So once you start this process, it is most important that you continue even and especially when there are signs of improvement.

Signs of feedback

Here are some of the 'feedback' signs which will indicate that change is taking place and that the process is working.

Social aspects of behaviour regarding feedback may include:

» Improvement in speech, movement, co-ordination, awareness.

» Improved memory and improved general health.

» Not influenced by peer group pressure and playing more with other children.

» Better comprehension of what is being said and communicated.

» Changes occurring with mood and self-esteem.

» Less shy and withdrawn, less aggressive and anxious.
» Calmer, less hypertensive and physically agitated.
» More energy and self-confidence.
» Sleeping better throughout the night and happier on awakening in the morning.
» Higher self-esteem and more periods in a positive mood.
» Changes in personal habits e.g. bed-wetting and nail-biting.
» Improved concentration, less attention-seeking behaviour.
» Less fearful and more self-reliant.
» More optimistic and less aggressive.

Family issues regarding feedback may include:
» Improved co-operation, accepting of hugs and terms of endearment.
» More responsive, communicates better and greater involvement with the family.
» Less argumentative and less conflict with siblings.
» Shares toys more with others, and less possessive.
» More loving, accepts and gives affection.
» Less secretive — more open in communication, shares thoughts more openly.
» Argues less with family members, accepts direction without argument.
» More involvement with activities at school or home and more agreeable.
» Improved eating habits.

School issues regarding feedback may include:
» Happier and more approachable at school.
» Less concern regarding school, studying, writing and reading.
» Improved results in extra-curricular activities.
» Less anxious regarding study.
» Increased concentration and attention.
» Less arguments regarding homework and assignments.
» Happy to get up in the morning.

What to do when you notice feedback

If you have noticed any changes in your child's behaviour, make no comment at this stage as it may cause your child to become self-conscious. Just be very supportive and positive in your approach.

To encourage feedback, you could ask, 'How are you today?' occasionally throughout the day. The answer may come back 'Happy'. Sometimes this can occur with an expression of amazement — because your child may be used to getting attention by showing unhappiness! How your child expresses new feelings can vary considerably. A favourite memory of mine is of a little girl whose feedback was: 'The fairies talk to me at night. They tell me they love me, and they sound just like mum!' Your child might even say unexpectedly, 'I love you, mum', which is fabulous 'feedback' especially if they don't usually say or express their feelings. Also watch for physical feedback — the child may give you a little hug or an unexpected cuddle — something out of the ordinary.

What if you don't notice feedback?

If you don't think you have received feedback, don't be concerned. It might mean that you have missed a few nights of SleepTalk™ or perhaps your child also needs your partner's involvement, or just that the 'feedback' is very subtle. It could be that your child is particularly anxious, so the more you work with the process and the fewer nights you miss, the quicker feedback will occur.

If you go out for an evening, then conduct SleepTalk™ upon your return. It may take a little longer to access the correct brain wave frequency, but it will still work. Remember not to whisper. The issue is not *if* you get feedback, but *when* you get feedback.

If 'feedback' does not occur after the first two months of the basic 'Foundation' process, here are some points to consider which may be delaying the results:

1. Have you followed the directions correctly? Check the process.

2. How many times have you actually performed the process? Have you missed some evenings?

3. Is there another primary carer or carers in your child's life? Can they contribute to the SleepTalk™ process?

4. Are you allowing the child the correct amount of time to settle before beginning the SleepTalk™ process?

5. Is there too much noise or interference around, such as radio or television? Are other children playing nearby?

6. Does your child have any intellectual difficulties or severe anxiety or stress? If so, SleepTalk™ feedback can take a little longer, especially with intellectually and/or physically impaired children.

7. If you are certain that you have followed the directions correctly, but are still waiting on results, contact me directly via the SleepTalk™ web site.

Using SleepTalk™ during the day

You may also use the 'Foundation' statements whilst your child is awake, for added reinforcement. For instance, when the child comes home from school just reiterate 'mummy loves you' or 'daddy loves you' or 'I love you'. Also be aware of how you can turn a negative statement into a positive one. For instance, instead of saying, 'Watch that cup of coffee, Mark, you're going to spill it', say something like, 'Mark, you are doing very well carrying that coffee, just walk slowly'. The positive statement would be much more powerful. I can remember saying to little Michelle, 'For goodness sake Michelle be careful with that cup of coffee, you'll drop it'. I didn't realise that I was actually suggesting to her that she would drop it!

As you work through the process you may also notice a very welcome side effect. Other children in the family and even your partner will often become happier and more co-operative as the energy of your child starts to change. This makes sense when one considers that if one member of a family is unhappy, unwell or insecure it can affect the whole family unit.

When you feel that the 'Foundation' process has been successful and that positive changes have begun to take place in your child, you may wish to introduce one or more of the 'Support' processes discussed later. But before that occurs make sure you have presented the 'Foundation' suggestions for at least three to four weeks.

Continued success!

It is absolutely vital that you understand the importance of continuity to the success of SleepTalk™, because it's similar to taking antibiotics: you notice improvement in your health, the symptoms have disappeared, so you discontinue the course of treatment and it's most likely that the symptoms will return, sometimes worse than before. In the same way, the SleepTalk™ process needs the continual reinforcement of the suggestions on a daily basis, over a set period of time, in order to ensure the desired results.

Having learned the theory of SleepTalk™ we come to the most important factor in implementing this process. Whatever the result you are seeking for your child, be prepared to continue the process for a minimum of three months: it will only work if you are diligent and persistent.

Your child's security

The 'Foundation' process gives your child a basic security and a feeling of wellbeing. Their increasingly positive self-image and confidence, how they feel about themselves and their place in the world will be of enormous value to them throughout their lives. Children have to walk their own pathway and the best that we can do as parents is to give them the skills, confidence and self-esteem to be able to deal with life's inevitable difficulties.

The law of attraction

I'm sure you have heard the saying 'like attracts like'. If you emanate love, if you emanate harmony, that's what will be attracted into your world. Conversely, if you emanate anger, resentment and disharmony, that discord and anger will be your world. Think about it, in reality it's *your* choice how you react to something. If you choose in the morning to be angry, then that's how you will deal with your world and that's how the world will deal with you. If you choose in the morning to be happy, then that's what you will attract. You might not be able to change a situation occurring in your life, a situation just *is*. If it's impossible to change it, then the only thing that you can change is your attitude towards it.

Day by day, in every way
It gets better and better
Emile Coué

SLEEPTALK™

chapter eight
Introducing the SleepTalk™ support process

ONCE THE BASIC 'FOUNDATION' PROCESS HAS BEEN ACCEPTED, you can address the child's individual needs or, as I call it, the 'Primary' area of need. These can be in the area of a difficulty or issues faced by the child, such as bed-wetting, fear or sibling rivalry. Or you may just wish to give your child some suggestions which will create a positive attitude in a particular area and encourage them to reach their goals, for instance, increase their confidence in sport, music and social situations.

Remember that the 'Foundation' process is designed to establish and reinforce a confident and positive self-image. This means that although the basic, underlying stress and anxiety responsible for unwelcome behaviour has been addressed, some difficulties may remain simply as a habit. For instance, after the 'Foundation' process has been accepted the habit of nail-biting may still exist even though the initial cause, which may have been anxiety, has been removed. The appropriate 'Support' process will usually help to break the habit.

Some parents are quite surprised to realise that their child's unwanted behaviour has in fact stemmed from a lack of self-esteem, particularly when the behaviour is aggressive, naughty or attention seeking. However, low self-esteem or a feeling of not being unconditionally loved can most certainly be the underlying cause!

Once the 'Foundation' suggestions were being accepted by Michelle it was necessary to determine the next stage. Because Michelle suffered from dyspraxia, speech was a very important issue. So to assist her speech we formulated specific suggestions which we incorporated into the basic 'Foundation' script.

For the next couple of months we included into the SleepTalk™ the additional suggestion, 'You can talk', then we progressed to, 'You can talk — you will talk — you are talking'. When feedback indicated an improvement in Michelle's speech — which took about a month — we then included, 'Your speech is improving day by day in every way. It's getting better every day in every way'. The word 'it' becomes very important to the mind when using SleepTalk™ because the mind will determine what the 'it' represents.

The suggestions that we included over a period of time covered many needs. Once we determined that Michelle's speech was improving we then concentrated on other areas of need. Over a long period of time suggestions that enabled her to develop the basic survival skills necessary for her to cope with her world were introduced into the SleepTalk™ script. They included, 'You can walk; 'you can talk; you enjoy going to school; you can write and draw; you are better and better every day; you are stronger every day in every way'. Michelle's needs were many and major so the suggestions were changed as feedback indicated acceptance. It took many years of patience for the full process to be implemented but the results were rewarding.

Michelle stayed at school until she was 21 and then moved into a sheltered workshop. I will always remember the comments the workshop supervisor made one day when discussing Michelle (remember she still only had an intellectual IQ of around 45). He said, 'What Michelle lacks in ability she more than makes up with effort.' Her nickname became 'chatter box'. She was always happy because if anything in her world was unacceptable to her or gave her concern she would literally go to bed and sleep! When she woke up, her world was happy and she was able to resume her activities.

Choosing the 'Primary' suggestions

Now let's take the first step in creating your action plan and select your child's 'Primary' area of need. Choose from the categories or area of need which you think will best help your child. Let's look at the different areas that may be relevant to your needs. They could include some of the following:

» Aggression or difficult behaviour
» Study or concentration
» Physical impairment or sports activity
» Health issues
» Creativity and co-operation
» Bed-wetting or nightmares
» Sibling rivalry
» Fear or anxiety
» Nail-biting
» Asthma or speech
» Achieving goals
» Skin disorders
» General issues
» Eating disorders

When choosing the 'Specific' area of need to be addressed always select the 'Primary' issues in your child's life. Don't be too concerned about the less important areas, because the energy or the behaviour relating to them will change as a result of addressing the most important and underlying issue. So having chosen the area of need that you would like to work with, you can then select up to three 'Support' suggestions within that category which you feel will suit your child the most. The complete 'Support' category suggestions you will find in the next chapter. These suggestions can be added, one at a time, to the 'Foundation' process over the next few weeks. Allow for feedback before introducing additional 'specific' suggestions.

Keep a record of both the category you have chosen as the 'Primary' area of need (remember to only select one) and the three 'Support' suggestions that you have chosen from that category. If you identify more than one 'Primary' area of need, remember that you must only work with one at a time. For instance, you may decide that confidence is the over-riding issue but there's also a nail-biting habit you want to deal with. Always wait for sufficient feedback or at least a month before progressing to an additional 'Primary' area.

One of the reasons is that the principal and most urgent 'Primary' area of need in this case — confidence — just might be the underpinning reason for the nail-biting. As the subconscious mind begins to accept suggestions for a positive self-image and confidence, the down line ramifications of change that occur may in fact help to reduce the nail bitting. Anxiety has reduced and confidence has increased.

Working with the first support suggestion

Now you are ready to begin to work with your first chosen 'Primary' area. Let's say that you have chosen 'Behaviour' from the list as your child's 'Primary' area of need. You will notice that two suggestions at the beginning of this list are identified by an asterisk or *. These have been chosen as the most appropriate suggestions to suit a wide range of situations within that category or 'Primary' area of need. However, you may decide to choose others within the category — that's fine. Record your selections on the 'Support' process chart on page 101.

Adding suggestions to the 'Foundation' process

The suggestions you have chosen will follow on from the 'Foundation' process you are already delivering each night. At the completion of the basic script, at the point where you would normally say, 'Deep asleep, deep asleep' , now introduce your first 'Support' suggestion, repeating it at least three times then closing as normal. Continue to deliver the first 'Support' suggestion until you begin to receive feedback, or for at least 21 days. The kind of feedback will be similar to that noticed during the 'Foundation' process.

Introducing the additional suggestions

When feedback is noticed and 21 days have passed after adding the first 'Support' suggestion to the 'Foundation' process, it's time to introduce your second suggestion selected from the list. Follow the same procedure as before, adding the second suggestion to the first which of course follows the basic. A third 'Support' suggestion is added when sufficient feedback is received from the second 'Support' suggestion.

In this way you are building the process. Even when you are delivering the 'Foundation' process plus two 'Support' suggestions, the entire thing will probably only take you about five minutes each night. Don't forget to record the feedback date and comments or activities you observe.

Continue with this process for at least three months. Keep noting feedback and if at the end of the first three months you are confident that the results have been achieved, you can safely move on to a new 'Primary' area of need. Do not discontinue the process when you notice improvement. Utilise this fabulous opportunity to further enhance your child's future. If you haven't received feedback within 21 days don't be concerned — just continue until you do. If you are in any doubt as to whether it's time to change the suggestions please contact me via the web site address.

Remember, the success of this process is entirely dependent on your commitment to deliver it every night for at least three months! Of course, there will be the odd occasion when you miss a night. Providing you have been generally consistent, this will not interfere with the process. Remember, it's not a matter of *if* this process works, but *when*.

Guidelines to ensure success

When working with the 'Support' process there are a number of guidelines which must be followed if full advantage is to be gained.

1. Language must always be suitable to the child's age and understanding.

Always select your suggestions using the language that is appropriate not only to the situation that you wish to address, but also to the age and understanding of the child. For instance, from the list of suggestions under 'General', on page 99, the statement, 'You are motivated and enthusiastic' or 'Your attitude to your family and friends is both positive and caring' would certainly suit a nine–ten year old and, depending on the individual, perhaps even a six–seven year old. However, the language is too sophisticated for a three or four year old. So for this age group, the suggestions could be, 'You are healthy, clever and love having fun', or 'we all love you'.

2. Reinforcement of suggestions throughout the day is essential.

Whatever suggestions you select in the 'Support' process and use each night, you must reinforce during the day using the same language, which will prevent any misunderstanding in the acceptance of this communication. The reinforcement to the conscious mind strengthens the total mind's acceptance of the ideas.

3. Always use positive language

When working with the 'Support' processes, it's most important that positive, rather than negative words are used. For instance, it's inappropriate to use the words 'never', 'no' or 'not'. If you're dealing with bed-wetting, you might be tempted to say, 'You will not wet the bed'. However, what actually happens is the mind will recognise and accept 'wet the bed' rather than the direction of the word 'not'. So in fact what you are doing is reinforcing the suggestion of 'wetting the bed' rather than 'not wet the bed'. For example, if I said to you, 'Don't think of an elephant', of course you thought of an elephant!

Reinforce the positive language throughout the day and keep a diary of what you say, the feedback and, when it occurs and how you felt about it.

4. Suggestions appropriate for life

Only use the suggestions on the 'Support' process list. These suggestions and scripts have been carefully worded to avoid inappropriate suggestions. For instance, a poorly worded suggestion may be just right at the time you deliver it, but as the child grows older, it may not be appropriate. Statements given to our children must always be appropriate — not just now, but for next month, next year and for always.

You will find that the recommended 'Support' suggestions can be used at any time: they are open ended, non-intrusive, safe and conflict will not occur if the suggestions are not accepted 100%. For example, the suggestion under the Sports section on page 97, 'You enjoy playing sports' has deliberately not included the words 'at school' or 'every day', so that as the child grows older the suggestion will still be powerful, even after leaving school when in a wider environment. Also you will notice that the suggestions do not use 'conditions' of any kind; saying for example, 'You will be happy tomorrow because the sun will be shining' may cause conflict if the sun did not shine the next day.

5. Getting to the underlying matter

Bear in mind, when choosing the areas in which you would most like your child to experience success, that sometimes a problem or issue expressed by your child may not in fact reflect the real underlying cause. For example, if your child says, 'I hate school', the real underlying issue may not be a dislike of school, but a problem with a teacher or peer group pressure. So try to talk to your child to elicit more information which will point to the underlying concern. You will then be able to choose a 'Support' suggestion most appropriate to the situation at hand. The issue may be more about confidence with their peer group than about hating school. You may wish to select the 'Support' process suggestions relating to 'Confidence' on page 94, which says, 'You're a fun person to be with'. You may add later the suggestion that 'you voice your opinion with confidence and calmness' or 'you enjoy making friends and are happy at school'.

If you are not sure about the underlying cause for the child saying they hate school, the suggestion highlighted with the asterisk will generally be enough to encompass the issue and therefore be successful.

6. Select only one support process at time

Remember to only select one 'Support' process suggestion to begin with. Continue to deliver this suggestion until you are noticing good feedback and at least 21 days have passed. Then follow on with the next suggestion, adding it always after the 'Foundation' suggestion and first 'Support' suggestion. A third suggestion may be added in the same way after the same period of time or after noticing sufficient feedback to tell you that the previous suggestions have been successful. After about three months of continued reinforcement, and only then, select another 'Primary' area of need and repeat the process.

7. Keeping your diary

Keep a diary to document the progress of SleepTalk™. It is very important to formally note the suggestions you use and the feedback signs on a daily basis. It will enable you to see a pattern forming and to ensure that signs of change do not go unnoticed. The best time to add to your diary is the end of the day, after you have delivered the evening process. The diary will also be very helpful should you need to discuss the process with someone — perhaps a professional therapist or teacher.

8. History of medical or psychological distress

If there is a history of medical or psychological distress, please discuss the use of SleepTalk™ with your medical practitioner or specialist. This is particularly important in dealing with children with a history of shock treatment, epilepsy, psychoses, deep depression or bipolar disorder.

9. What if I say something wrong during the process?

Many times parents have expressed concern about the wording for SleepTalk™: it must be accurate and it's important to carefully follow the script. My reply is always to reassure them that SleepTalk™ can do no harm. While most parents have made inappropriate comments in the past, SleepTalk™ enables correction because it's non-intrusive and loving. The primary and most rewarding aspect of this comment is the realisation of the power that all communications have, and the importance of always making positive rather than negative comments.

10. Use in conjunction with other therapies

SleepTalk™ is a process which may be used in conjunction with psychotherapy, or indeed any other form of therapy or assistance which the child may be receiving. Studies and case histories over the past 30 years have demonstrated the effectiveness of SleepTalk™ either as a primary procedure or as an adjunct to other treatments. But remember that children do not necessarily have to be experiencing a 'problem' to benefit from SleepTalk™. In fact, students desiring higher marks at school, or perhaps increased concentration, may benefit. Sometimes SleepTalk™ has been the catalyst, allowing other therapies to work. Similar to compound interest, one initial aspect allows additional and previous learning to become accepted and acted upon. Nothing works in isolation.

When I first began to share this process with other parents, a common response was, 'It's like a miracle — it really does work!' Persevere with this safe yet dynamic process, and you will experience your own wonderful miracle. SleepTalk™ is such a simple yet direct program you can become involved in, resulting in shared experience, purpose and achievement.

Over the past years a number of parents have discussed with me the difficulty they have experienced when saying to their child 'I love you'. A number of reasons have been offered for this, the most frequent being fear of rejection. When using the SleepTalk™ process parents sometimes find they are able to express their emotions without inhibition and fear of rejection. Some fathers have also mentioned that they were brought up to believe men do not say, 'I love you' to their sons, or even allow their emotions to show. Conversely, some parents become angry at the suggestion that their child may not believe that they are unconditionally loved. Many times I have heard the line, 'But my children know I love them, look what I do for them'. Well folks, that's not the point — saying the actual words is the important part.

May I ask you to consider remembering the emotions felt when someone said to you, 'I love you'? When was the last time you said to someone close to you, 'I love you'. Children especially need to subconsciously *know* that they are loved, even when they have been naughty. That it was their behaviour you were rejecting, not them! The following chapter details the suggestions that you can use.

chapter nine

Selecting the 'Primary' area of need

The 'Support' suggestions must now be carefully chosen. The major issue that you wish to work with is selected first and the back-up additional suggestions are then added. At the end of this chapter, on page 101, you will find an example of a support process chart, and one for you to use.

For this example the 'Primary' area is 'Behaviour'. Notice that I have entered 'Behaviour' next to and on the same line as the 'Primary' area of need. Enter your selection making sure you read all the examples first. The first 'Support' suggestion chosen is also entered along with the date commenced. I selected, 'You are calm, confident and self assured'. Notice there is a place for you to record both the date and any observed feedback. The feedback I recorded was, 'Pat played really happily today' and, 'Pat didn't lose his temper when arguing with Tom today'.

When it is time to select the second 'Support' suggestion just follow the same procedure. Always remember to read all the way through the offered suggestions before you make your choice.

It can be a complicated procedure to formulate appropriate statements regarding the primary issues, so I have provided a selection of statements which might assist. However, I strongly recommend that you select only those that are identified within the sections.

The first two statements in each section are identified with an asterisk because I consider them to be of exceptional value. However, you may prefer to use the alternative statements, as long as you help your child understand the terminology by repeating the statements throughout the day.

Confidence/Anxiety

* You are confident, positive and calm.
* Whatever you do today, you will do with confidence and security.
» It's OK to be you. You are intelligent and happy.
» You have strength of mind and a confident attitude.
» Whatever the day brings, you remain calm, positive and in control of your thoughts and emotions.
» You can succeed, you are successful.
» You are calm, relaxed and secure within yourself.
» You voice your opinion with confidence and calmness.
» You are a fun person to be with.
» You express your opinions calmly and with confidence.
» You are safe.

Goal Achievement

* You achieve to the best of your own personal ability.
* You can, you will, you are achieving your goals.
» Regardless of what occurs today you handle it calmly and efficiently to the best of your ability.
» You enjoy achieving.
» It's OK to win.

Speech

* ❊ You can talk, you will talk, you are talking.
* ❊ You turn thoughts into words easily.
* ❊ It's OK for you to talk.
* » You speak and act with confidence.
* » You speak fluently, easily and well.
* » You are able to express your thoughts and feelings easily.
* » You are in total control of your voice.
* » When you talk you remain calm and speak clearly.
* » Your speech gets better and better every day in every way.
* » You are able to communicate your needs clearly.
* » You are talking clearly and easily and without hesitation.
* » You express your opinions calmly and with confidence.
* » It's getting better and better every day in every way.

Behaviour — Bullying

* ❊ You can control your behaviour.
* ❊ You are calm, confident and self-assured.
* » You behave in a socially acceptable manner.
* » Your ability to cope with family and friends gets better and better.
* » Your co-operation and attitude is positive.
* » Life is exciting and fun.
* » You enjoy being with others.
* » You are happy to share and communicate with others.
* » You treat others as you would like to be treated.

Study

* ❊ Learning is good, interesting and fun.
* ❊ You enjoy school, making friends and learning.
* » You enjoy learning new things.
* » Your memory, concentration, comprehension and attitude is getting better and better every day in every way.
* » You are creative and talented.
* » Your mind is calm and receptive to learning.

» You enjoy making friends and are happy at school and/or study.
» You enjoy maths, reading, writing, spelling.
» Your attention to detail is getting better and better.
» Your study habits are organised and focused.
» Study is becoming easier and easier.
» You voice your opinion with confidence and calmness.
» You enjoy study.
» Your concentration, comprehension and listening skills are getting better and better every day in every way.
» Your recall is getting better and better.
» You express what you know in words clearly and easily.
» You enjoy reading books.

Physical

✲ You can, you will, you are ... walking (select the activity).
✲ You're getting better and better every day in every way.
✲ It's OK for you to walk.
✲ It's OK for you to talk.
» You can walk.
» You can run.
» Your co-ordination is improving.
» It (the activity) gets better and better.
» You retain your balance.
» You are becoming stronger day by day in every way.

Health

✲ 'It' gets better and better every day in every way.
✲ Your body knows how to heal itself.
» You are happy, healthy and successful.
» You are now experiencing perfect health.
» You are growing healthy and strong.

Creativity and Expression

* ❖ You are able to express your thoughts and ideas with clarity.
* ❖ You express yourself freely.
* » You are talented.
* » You are creative.
* » Your creativity is getting stronger and stronger.
* » You have good ideas which you are comfortable sharing.

Sports

* ❖ You can, you will, you are doing really well.
* ❖ You will and are achieving your best.
* » You can win.
* » It's OK to win.
* » You are winning.
* » You're getting better and better every day.
* » You enjoy playing sports.
* » You have a happy, positive, confident and healthy attitude.
* » See also *General* list

Bed-wetting (Enuresis)

Before working with this issue we need to discuss a few things. Bed-wetting can be linked to fear, or in some cases fear of an authority figure, e.g. a teacher at school. Be sensitive to the possibility and try to identify the issues and or the authority person. If you feel it may possibly be fear of the father image, it's most important that the male primary-care giver gives SleepTalk™ and involves himself with the positive auto-suggestions during the waking state.

Always make sure any physical problems have been medically eliminated. Consider also the possibility that the bed-wetting is just a habit, or too much/too early potty training.

* ❖ When you need to go the toilet — you wake, walk to the toilet, puddle/toilet/wee in the toilet, return to bed and go to sleep.
* ❖ You wake when you need to puddle/toilet/wee.
* » You are confident and safe within.
* » See also *Confidence, Anxiety, Fear,* and *General list.*

Sibling Rivalry

❖ We all love you.

❖ Your brother/sister loves you.

» You are very special to your brother/sister.

» Your brother/sister are very special to you.

» You enjoy your family.

» You are an important member of the family.

Fear and Anxiety

❖ You are safe, secure and loved.

❖ You are confident.

» You are calm, relaxed and secure within yourself.

» See also *Confidence* and *General list*.

Nail-biting

This may be a major symptom of anxiety or simply a nervous habit. There may be a situation your child feels incapable of handling e.g. school, exams, relationships. Try to identify the problem but do not remove the *effect* without knowing the *cause*. If you suspect that it is a symptom of anxiety try on a conscious level to identify the cause and then address the anxiety related to that cause. If it's just a learned behaviour pattern or a habit always repeat the suggested terminology during waking hours and only use words that can be understood.

❖ Your nails are strong and healthy.

❖ Your nails are growing longer and longer.

» You allow your nails to grow strong and healthy.

» You enjoy having strong, healthy nails.

» You are confident, self assured and calm within.

» Your nails are improving/gaining in health and length.

Asthma

Fear and/or anxiety can in many cases be the initial cause of asthma. It is also wise to eliminate the possibility of allergies. Of course, always consult your health practitioner. The following suggestions may be useful.

* ❖ You breathe freely and easily.
* ❖ Your lungs get stronger and stronger every day in every way.
* » You are confident and safe within.
* » Your breathing gets better and better every day in every way.
* » You are able to breathe more freely.
* » You are enjoying exercising and swimming.
* » You are strong and in harmony with your world.
* » You are calm and in control.

Skin

* ❖ Your skin is healthy and clear.
* ❖ Your skin grows healthy and clear.
* » You are beautiful (handsome) and intelligent.
* » It's getting better and better.
* » Your skin is soft and without blemishes.
* » You eat foods that are good for your skin.

General

* ❖ You can, you will, you are.
* ❖ We all love you.
* » Your sister/brother loves you.
* » You enjoy your family.
* » You enjoy change.
* » Your health is good.
* » You eat the correct foods for you.
* » Your self-confidence is getting stronger and stronger.
* » You are enjoying playing sport.
* » You enjoy winning.
* » Your attitude to family and friends is positive and caring.
* » Your health is getting better and better.

» You sleep deeply and soundly.
» Your dreams are safe.
» You are motivated and enthusiastic.
» You are happy, healthy, clever and accepted.
» You are clever, healthy and love having fun.

Eating

The focus should be on good nutrition and sensible eating patterns, not on weight loss or gain. If your child has expressed concern about body image, it would be more appropriate to give suggestions relating to confidence than to tackle these issues directly. It is also inappropriate to say, 'You will eat all the food on your plate', or offer an incentive such as sweets if all the food is eaten. Never use persuasion as there might come a time when that suggestion is inappropriate, such as with the development of hypoglycaemia or diabetes. Please consult a medical specialist, health consultant or natural therapist if you are concerned that your child has a weight problem. If you suspect that your child has anorexia make sure that a good quality, liquid vitamin B group combination is given — and consult a medical practitioner.

You will find a link on the SleepTalk™ web page to a number of different organisations that may be able to assist you with nutritional information. The following suggestions relating to diet should only be selected if there is an *absence of physical and/or emotional distress.* However, less specific suggestions selected from other groups may assist — if in doubt, contact me via the web or by email.

✻ You eat only foods which are correct for you.
✻ You enjoy foods which are good, healthy and nourishing.
» You control your desire for snack foods.
» You eat sensibly and in sensible amounts.
» You only eat the foods that are healthy for you.

Example only — next two pages
Support Process Chart:

Example only

Date Commenced	First Primary Area of Need Selected **Behaviour**	Date Feedback Observed	Feedback Observed & Comments made
Introduced Date: / /	Enter first support suggestion *You are calm, confident and self-assured*	Enter date you first noticed change	Pat played really happily today. Pat didn't lose his temper when arguing with Tom today.
Introduced Date: / /	Enter second support suggestion *You are well behaved*		Pat made his bed today without argument. No complaints from the baby-sitter.
Introduced Date: / /	Enter third support suggestion *You can control your behaviour*		Teacher commented on improved behaviour. Made a new friend today.
	Second Primary Area of Need Selected **Sibling Rivalry**		
Introduced Date: / /	Enter first support suggestion *Your brother loves you*		John didn't argue with his brother today. He helped him with his homework.
Introduced Date: / /	Enter second support suggestion *You are an important member of the family*		John lent his brother his bike and helped him. The boys are starting not to fight over the TV.
Introduced Date: / /	Enter third support suggestion *Your brother is very special to you*		School commented that John is much calmer and attentive at school. He is playing better and is less anxious, not so competitive.

For your records

Date Commenced	First Primary Area of Need Selected **Behaviour**	Date Feedback Observed	Feedback Observed & Comments made
Introduced Date: / /	Enter first support suggestion		
Introduced Date: / /	Enter second support suggestion		
Introduced Date: / /	Enter third support suggestion		
	When completely sure you have achieved the changes required then select the next 'Primary' area of concern	Enter date	Enter the comments of observed behaviour as before
	Second Primary Area of Need Selected		
Introduced Date: / /	Enter first support suggestion		
Introduced Date: / /	Enter second support suggestion		
Introduced Date: / /	Enter third support suggestion		

chapter ten

Frequently asked questions

WE HAVE DISCUSSED THE BASIC PRINCIPLES, the 'Fundamental' processes and the selection of 'Primary' area of need. Feedback has been documented and the recording of specific progress was facilitated using the Support Progress chart.

Now that you have had an opportunity to work with the SleepTalk™ process it might help to clarify some issues if I share the following questions and answers with you. Throughout workshops and lectures I have given over the years a number of questions always seem to arise, so I have included a few to assist with clarification.

Q.	*Does it matter if only one parent conducts SleepTalk™?*
A.	It's much better for both parents to be involved. It's less effective if only one parent is, but only marginally. With approximately 30 years of case evidence to work from, albeit anecdotal, different levels of improvement occurred. It was evident that it's much more efficient if both parents are involved because it balances the energy of the male/female, the mum/dad component within the child's perception. The child receives their basic self-image, self-worth and sense of balance from both

parents and it is, in my opinion, most important for that child to have a sense of acceptance and unconditional love from both. Of course, problems can arise if there is difficulty of access to one of the parents. Resentment and anger and all those other human emotions can come into the equation but basically, if at all possible, it's far better for children to have a sense of self-worth and self-acceptance from both parents. If it is difficult to include both, just use the term, 'We all love you'.

Q. *When there is a stepmother or father, what happens to the basic script regarding the absent 'biological' partner?*

A. As with the previous question, this can be a very emotive issue and in some cases it's appropriate to just say, 'Mummy loves you, daddy loves you, we all love you'. The child's basic self-image comes from both parents and it's important that children are comfortable loving both parents without guilt. If there is a mother and a stepfather, children may feel anxious, guilty or even disloyal loving the stepfather. They may believe that they shouldn't love dad any more because it might be disloyal to the stepfather; confusion can result, with feelings of guilt or helplessness. Thoughts like, 'It's my fault daddy or mummy has left' may come in to the picture. Children sometimes feel that to love one parent is to be disloyal to the other. For your child's needs to be met it's important that they receive love from both parents without guilt. If this issue is inappropriately dealt with then great confusion can result, and guilt may become a component of your child's emotions. If they are given a message of fear or hate from one parent, or they are subjected to negative comments about the other parent, the only result will be confusion and disharmony, fear and helplessness, which may develop into aggression and anger.

Q. *What happens if the non-custodial parent is restricted in terms of access? Doesn't that cause conflict if I use SleepTalk™?*

A. No. The SleepTalk™ process will in fact assist your child to manage their world. It's not SleepTalk™ that causes conflict, it's disharmony within the family structure and the influences within the family home. How do you overcome it? By saying, 'mummy loves you, daddy loves you, we all love you ...' — statements which may be difficult for parents who hate each other; such disharmony can very easily be expressed in the way they speak about each other. Children form an opinion as a result of the emotions which are reflected in the voice. The result of SleepTalk™ would be to allow or establish a sense of security and confidence within your child's mind. If SleepTalk™ is introduced the child accepts the fact that they are loved by mum or dad regardless. SleepTalk™ is about reinforcing the acceptance of self-worth, self-confidence and a positive self-esteem of 'I am unconditionally loved'. In other words SleepTalk™ is about utilising the potential within the child, allowing an understanding and acceptance that they are unconditionally loved by their parents, notwithstanding the fact that one of the parents is absent. They may have left home, died, or established another family unit. Sometimes, it's appropriate to try and deal with this particular issue from an intellectual viewpoint rather than an emotive one. The needs of the child must be paramount, regardless of conflict between the parents.

Q. *What happens if one parent doesn't love the child? Aren't you lying to the child?*

A. What gives you the right to assume the other parent or absent partner doesn't love the child? What right do parents have to tell a child that the other parent doesn't love them? Whether they have left the family unit, died or run off with someone, what right do they have to tell a child that the other parent doesn't love them? On the contrary, the custodial parent should reinforce the fact that of course the other parent loves them, whether they believe it to be true or not. The non-custodial parent may not be paying maintenance, may not be seeing the child, may even appear to be ignoring the child by not acknowledge birthdays or Christmas, but that doesn't automatically mean they don't love their child. It may be fact that they don't want anything to do with the child, but that's not what the little child's mind should be told. What other than resentment and anger would make a parent say such things?

If the child has the self-image of being loved by both parents and later finds out they weren't, at least they will be able to consider the situation with a positive self-image. To me, that's better than telling a child that they are not loved. It's inappropriate for one person to presume to know that another person doesn't love someone; they are not privileged to that information. It's only an assumption which is probably based on fear, certainly not on love.

Q. *What happens when marriages break up or one parent dies? The remaining parent is left very pre-occupied with their own resentment, hurt or guilt and they may tell negative stories about the parent who has gone. They try to put blame on to the other parent. What happens when, if they're conducting SleepTalk™ and are meant to say, 'Mummy loves you, daddy loves you', yet previously they may have said, 'Well daddy has left us ... and he's not coming back, he didn't love us any more ... ' What happens then?*

A. Whether dad or mum love the child now is really immaterial. The basic self-image of the child is the issue. When you are dealing with a great deal of resentment and anger, it is important to address and recognise the issues involved; whether the parent loved the child or not is immaterial. What is important is that the child believes that they are loved; continued negative suggestions only cause disharmony within the child's mind.

It is important that parents be aware of the down line

ramifications of such negative and destructive suggestions. We all like to know that we are loved, even though one parent may no longer be in the family environment. We never know what's going on in another person's mind, though we must be sure that the child has the basic self-belief and self-worth that creates unconditional love from both parents, regardless of whether it is true or not. Obviously, there might be a couple of exceptions, which we will talk about later, but in most cases, it's important that children gain a basic self-image and belief of being loved from both parents.

Q. *So what you are really saying is that it really doesn't matter whether, in reality, both parents love or loved the child. The important issue is that the child has the belief and self-image concept that they were loved and in fact are loved. Is that what you are saying?*

A. Yes, basically. It is not always possible for both parents to continually tell their child that they are loved. It might be physically impossible, because of separation, death or formation of another family unit. Or it may be physically impossible for them to communicate with the child. The issue is that the child has the belief and therefore the basic self-image of being loved by both parents without feeling guilty or disloyal in accepting that love from both parents.

Q   *If a parent is not living with the family and has previously abused the child either physically or emotionally — do you still say 'daddy loves you, mummy loves you'? Does the child interpret their behaviour (the behaviour of the so-called loving parent) as OK?*

A   If it is inappropriate to mention the absent parent by name, you could substitute, ' ... we all love you', instead of including a name or label. This allows the individual child to decide who 'we' represents in their mind. Remember that SleepTalk™ is not a therapy; it merely assists children to develop a positive 'I'm OK' belief and the confidence to say 'no'. In the case of an abused child, individual needs must always be addressed by a qualified professional.

Q   *Could you use the suggestion, 'You love yourself' during SleepTalk™?*

A.   Yes, but remember that as the SleepTalk™ process starts to be accepted by the subconscious mind, the aspect of self-love becomes an automatic response.

Q.   *What about dysfunctional families? Things occurring that we don't know about? For example, where the father or mother is abusing a child and the other parent doesn't know? What happens then?*

A.   This is of course a very difficult situation. SleepTalk™ suggestions give children the strength and support to deal with that type of issue in a very positive, rather than negative, or helpless, manner. At the very least children develop the confidence to deal with it and to say 'No'.

Children are empowered by SleepTalk™. The confidence and strength they gain enables them to confront and deal with issues. Children sometimes assume a personal sense of guilt and lack the confidence to deal with situations. SleepTalk™ assists children to develop confidence and as an extra bonus, parents develop an understanding regarding the use of suggestion. As a result, awareness of their issues and their behaviours may help to facilitate necessary change within the family unit. It's important that we don't make judgements, but conversely it's an issue that's becoming increasingly vocalised and one that we do have to deal with.

We need to recognise that children may be confused about the meaning of the word 'love'. Love can be a word used both as a negative weapon and a positive tool. However, if the basic SleepTalk™ suggestions are applied, the child can establish a self-confidence and the ability to deal with situations in a more confident manner. SleepTalk™ is a process that assists both children and parents. Information, education, knowledge and awareness can be major tools in combating inappropriate behaviour; 'knowing' can become a turning point for the parent, enabling them to deal with issues that they are trying to come to terms with. SleepTalk™ is a self-help process which empowers parents to assist their children to utilise the potential within and to gain a positive structure of belief and self-image for life.

Q. *Does SleepTalk™ work with children who don't have concerns or problems? And what benefits would they gain?*

A. Absolutely. Yes. SleepTalk™ is for all children. The recipients of SleepTalk™ do not necessarily have to have issues or problems. Children may be five or six years old, happy and well adjusted — but are you absolutely sure that they will continue to have a positive self-confidence as they grow and develop into adulthood? Many children grow up with a positive, healthy self-image without anxiety, but don't achieve their goals or individual potential. What a marvellous opportunity that parents have to stop the thieves of self-esteem.

Q. *What about asthma? Can SleepTalk™ assist?*

A. In some cases, yes. Asthma can be a physiological reaction to a psychological state of fear so the fear component of the asthma may have to be addressed. SleepTalk™ will help, but a referral to an appropriate therapist would be advisable. Because asthma can sometimes be caused by fear of life, death or even a major state of anxiety, simple suggestions such as those included in the 'Primary' suggestions can be helpful. SleepTalk™ is not presented as a panacea for all problems, but can certainly be utilised in conjunction with other modalities for all situations.

Q. *In previous discussions you commented that it's not appropriate to use persuasion with SleepTalk™. Why is that?*

A. Using persuasion causes problems. For example, 'You will be happy today because it is a school holiday' could cause conflict and disharmony when school holidays end because you have created a situation where the child believes that they will only be happy during holidays.

Q.   *What happens if my child is fine except for nail-biting?*
A.   There are a number of issues needing to be addressed here. Is the nail-biting just a habit, a learned behaviour, or perhaps a symptom of anxiety? Be very careful not to remove the actual biting of the nails without trying to determine or at least becoming aware of the possible cause. Removing the problem of nail-biting without finding the cause may cause your child to develop another symptom as a replacement. However the basic 'Foundation' belief of 'I'm OK' will cut in, reducing the level of anxiety (a possible cause) and as a consequence the reaction (in this case nail-biting) is reduced. The subconscious mind accepts the suggestions and develops a belief system of 'I'm OK, I'm loved, I can handle this'. As a result the nail-biting which was the effect of distress, anxiety or bad self-image will just become a learned behaviour pattern as the anxiety becomes reduced. The basic belief of 'I'm OK' is reinforced and the down-line ramifications of the process are profound. The nail-biting, or asthma — as we discussed before — may have been issues because they didn't feel 'OK' about themselves. Now they do, and the habit has changed. If this is the case, the particular benefit of using the specific suggestions after the basic SleepTalk™ process will instigate behavioural change. It's as simple as that.

Q.   *Can you work with multiple issues at the same time?*
A.   No. My advice is that you don't try. Work with the basic 'Foundation' process until you have the feedback that the suggestions are accepted, then you can start working with the specifics, but only one at a time. Don't demand too much of the subconscious mind. Determine the 'Primary' area of need or the specific issue. Your child may be fearful of the weather or perhaps going to school? Determine the main rather than the minor issues e.g. they can't do up their shoe laces, don't keep their bedroom tidy, or don't eat meals properly. These are secondary issues which will change as your child gradually develops basic self-confidence and self-image. Remember that

low self-esteem, anxiety, lack of confidence, a feeling of 'I'm not OK' and 'life's a bit suspect', will all change with the acceptance of the 'I'm OK' structure of the basic SleepTalk™ process.

Q. *Is there a specific suggestion you would use if a child was anxious about going to school?*

A. Yes, there is. I would select from the 'Study' and 'Confidence-Anxiety' suggestions. Again, this indicates a lack of confidence and a very anxious state of mind. It may be appropriate to select from the 'General' section also. It really depends on the individual child and the circumstances. Try to determine the reasons for the anxiety.

Q. *What happens if they have a fear of someone?*

A. A very difficult question and very important. Never use the suggestion, 'You will not be frightened of your teacher'. You may find that down the line, it's appropriate to be frightened of the teacher. With SleepTalk™ it's not always necessary to identify the cause or reason behind a fear. Remember that SleepTalk™ is not a therapy. Never give a suggestion that twenty years down the track might be inappropriate. Always make sure that the SleepTalk™ suggestions that are used will be appropriate at all times. By now you are aware how important it is to make sure that the suggestions you give your child, whether as 'waking' suggestions or SleepTalk™, are appropriate. Always be aware of what you are saying because the power of suggestion is huge. Take care what you say and how you say it.

Q. *How would you describe a child who awakens very easily, has difficulty going to sleep, or is often awake throughout the night?*

A. Very anxious. SleepTalk™ should be able to help but it may be difficult the first week or so to actually access the deep subconscious mind. The child may be fitful or have difficulty going to sleep or possibly wakes easily. If you persist with

SleepTalk™ the child will gain a sense of confidence. The anxiety will be reduced each time you use the SleepTalk™ process because you will be reinforcing a basic self-image and a belief that 'It's OK' and hopefully you will eventually also get a good night's sleep! By reducing the state of anxiety you gradually create for your child a new positive belief system and self-image. A distressed or anxious child will gradually accept the positive suggestions; their anxiety reduces and as a consequence the mind becomes more receptive to positive suggestions. Remember, you can never eliminate a memory, but you can add to it, alter or change the energy of that memory. Positive suggestions will eventually become more powerful than negative ones.

Q. *If a child has a basic negative belief structure and feels 'I'm not OK, I can't do something, I'm not as good as someone else', won't the SleepTalk™ process create confusion?*

A. Possibly, but only initially. Confusion would be a result of the 'positive' SleepTalk™ suggestions beginning to over-ride the accepted 'negative' suggestions within the subconscious mind. You may be aware of the process called 'Psycho-Cybernetics' developed by Maxwell Maltz who discusses the fact that it takes up to 21 days for the acceptance of a change of thought. SleepTalk™ is very similar. Over a period of time the new 'positive' thoughts start to build, becoming more powerful, diluting the energy of the 'I'm not OK' beliefs.

Information accepted by the subconscious mind is stored as fact alongside any previously accepted beliefs. What happens if we give the mind, the memory bank of belief, a positive suggestion such as, 'Mummy loves you, daddy loves you, it will be a happy day today', and that positive suggestion is positioned directly alongside a negative, 'I'm not OK' suggestion? Remember the 'Top Hat' process earlier? You will recall that repeating the initial suggestions of 'stay asleep — stay asleep' was to ensure the conscious part of the mind would continue

Q. *What about a very young child. How early can you start SleepTalk™?*

A. Basically I have answered this question earlier, but let's consider it in more detail. When does a child understand language? Young children may understand something by the tone of what is being said rather than actual words, equating calm, comforting words with whether they were being loved or not. The tone of what you say may in fact be enough to reach the understanding as even very small children can discern the difference between love and fear.

Q. *Would the subconscious mind understand, prior to birth, emotion coming from the mother?*

A. I think that would depend on your personal philosophy of whether or not you believe there's a connection of 'minds' prior to a child's birth. Some people believe — and I might add that I'm one of them — that prior to birth children have a level of awareness that has intelligence and the ability to understand, some say from a higher sense. I will leave that issue for the individual to determine. I personally think that the SleepTalk™ process can be used with a child of a very young age.

Q. *Is there any difference in the basic process when working with a 'normal' child to working with a child who has an intellectual, physical or emotional impairment?*

A. I've never really met a 'normal' child! The difference between what is considered normal or abnormal behaviour is society driven, defined by what the majority consider as 'normal', acceptable behaviour or standards. These can change because all children have conflicts and all children have the potential for improvement and the ability to utilise and be empowered by change. It just takes some children a little longer for the subconscious mind to fully accept suggestions and then express the reality of that belief. With a so-called 'normal' child allow up to three weeks, though sometimes it even happens in two–three days. Time frames change when working with a physically or intellectually impaired child. Be attuned to your child: the changes due to SleepTalk™ may initially be very subtle and can manifest themselves in a number of different ways.

Feedback is important, so wait for the belief to be accepted before attempting to build on it. For children who are physically, intellectually or emotionally impaired, be aware it may take much longer than three weeks for change to occur, which is why you must keep motivated.

Q. *What happens if dad or mum feels uncomfortable working with the process?*

A. Mums tend to be more in favour or perhaps more comfortable with the process, and some dads tend to be reluctant, especially the older generation. Perhaps the reason for this is a reluctance or difficulty to share or show emotions especially those born before the '50's and '60's. Later generations now accept that it's OK for a guy to go to his son and give him a hug and kiss and say, 'Gee I love you' especially in most western societies. However, in some cultures or countries it's inappropriate to hug another male even if that male is a child.

The SleepTalk™ process allows for both parents to share or display their feelings, thoughts and emotions in a safe environment without fear of rejection and without having to deal with personal self-image, perceived difficulties relating to interpersonal relationships or communication concerns.

Q. *Would you explain in more detail what you mean by 'feedback'?*

A. After about seven days of SleepTalk™ ask a direct question during the day such as, 'How are you today Johnny?', and he might say 'happy' — a recognised feedback statement or change of attitude. It may take longer so persist each night with the process and you will gradually see a subtle change. A shy little hug or changes in the way they speak, act, respond. They may appear calmer, happier, less anxious or shy. This is what we classify as feedback.

Q. *Would you tell the child that you are working with SleepTalk™ with them?*

A. With the younger children, no. Critical analysis may interfere and negate your efforts, but I would encourage the basic suggestions to be repeated during the waking hours to reinforce the process. It's one thing for dad to say '*I love you*' or '*daddy loves you*' whilst sitting on the end of the bed where no-one can hear or see, but it might not be quite so easy during the waking state, especially if they have a sense of discomfort.

Q. *What happens when children wake up during the basic SleepTalk™ process?*

A. Not a problem, just continue with the basic steps even if they sit up and look at you; or they may say to you in a sleepy voice, 'Go away, what are you doing?', or 'I love you too, mum'. They may even agree with you and nod as you work through the process. Any communication, movement or change is feedback, so don't be deterred. Just continue with the script because you are still accessing the deep subconscious.

Q. *Does it matter if the radio or the TV is on whilst conducting SleepTalk™?*

A. Yes, it does matter. It's important that televisions, radios, communication or conversations of any kind do not occur during SleepTalk™. You're accessing the deep subconscious mind so any aural interference may be confused with the suggestions that you giving.

Q. *My child is always happy. So how do I know if feedback is occurring?*

A. You need to be very sensitive if your child is always happy. Allow at least 21 days to ensure the basic process has been accepted before you start working on any 'Primary' area of need. Subtle feedback will be available if you tune into it. The feedback may include increased calmness, less anxiety, more confidence or just a change of attitude. Watch and observe!

Q. *When children are old enough to comprehend the death of a parent does that parent still get named?*

A. Yes. The fact that a parent has died does not alter their love. It is most important for children to believe and grow with the knowledge of the love of the deceased parent, who is still an essential component of the child's world. It's important the child believes the parent still loves them. That's the primary issue here, the child's belief that they are loved, regardless of whether or not the parent is present. Children's self-identity and security is balanced with the belief of love and acceptance of both parents without guilt.

Q. *Is SleepTalk™ the same as hypnosis?*

A. No. The only thing SleepTalk™ and hypnosis have in common is the use of suggestions. Hypnosis is conducted while you're awake with conscious memory of the process. SleepTalk™ is conducted whilst children are asleep with no conscious memory of the process.

Q. *Can I use SleepTalk™ during afternoon naps?*

A. Yes if you feel it necessary, especially if difficulty is experienced at sleep time. Usually, however, the night-time process is sufficient.

Q. *What happens if two children share a room?*

A. Try to work with each one independently.

Q. *Do I mention their names, singling them out?*

A. Yes. Certainly mention their names individually, especially when working with twins, because they are individual children.

Q.   *Can I use the child's name during SleepTalk™?*

A.   It is important that the child knows you are referring to them because it will help to maximise the benefits of SleepTalk™.

Q.   *What if both parents are involved in conducting SleepTalk™, do both do SleepTalk™ on the same evening?*

A.   Parents or primary carers need to alternate each evening.

Q.   *What happens when there is no reaction. Do I go ahead anyway or try later?*

A.   Persevere until you get a reaction which indicates transference. It may just be that the child is in a very deep sleep state, e.g. Delta. Eventually they will respond but yes, you could return later and try again.

My heart beats to the rhythm of love.
Louise Hay

chapter eleven

Down-line ramifications of change

THE SLEEPTALK™ PROCESS IF CONDUCTED CORRECTLY and consistently will develop a sense of closeness with your child. You may already have that closeness, which is great, but for many there can be a sense of separation and lack of understanding, feelings of rejection and hurt. Perhaps the 'bonding' process did not occur as expected. When some parents use the SleepTalk™ process it is as though they are being given a second chance to start over, to re-establish that bond or to re-establish that feeling of closeness, that feeling of love. If there has been anger, hurt, resentment or misunderstandings in communication, utilizing the process of SleepTalk™ can sometimes be a bridge to help reinforce the child's basic belief and acceptance of unconditional love. In some cases it helps to reinforce that it's the child's behaviour that you reject not the child.

It can be very difficult for some parents to express emotions. SleepTalk™ offers a safe and secure way for some parents to be able to actually say the words, 'I love you'. There are many reasons why it can be difficult to tell someone how you feel, perhaps because of fear of rejection or fear of being laughed at. Sometimes dads have difficulty in expressing emotion or repeating the basic foundation script of 'mummy loves you, daddy loves you'. For anyone to know that those statements would be accepted without rejection is a very rewarding experience. It is an exercise that somehow helps to build our own self-confidence as parents. Dad or mum might feel a little self conscious or silly sitting at the end of the bed talking to a sleeping child. SleepTalk™ is a process that empowers parents to be able to express deep emotions of unconditional love without fear of rejection and for the child to accept that unconditional love. As a result the family unit benefits because the down-line ramifications of change that occurs, encompasses and affects the entire family.

As you receive feedback, the interactions between your child and family members will change and inappropriate behaviour within the family structure will diminish. The symptoms of anxiety, resentment, hurt or stress will decrease and the down-line ramifications will create a positive reaction. As a consequence of accepting a belief structure of 'I'm OK, I'm confident', changes within the family are two-fold. Your response to changes in behaviour, energy and reactions creates a ripple effect and as a consequence the child responds to your change of attitude. The saying 'what comes round goes round' is apt. Action causes reaction and that reaction is expressed in the reduction of anxiety, concern and stress within the family structure.

It is important that the SleepTalk™ process is conducted with all children within the family as long as they are within the appropriate age range. Conduct SleepTalk™ with every child, whether you believe they have a need or not. Can you be absolutely sure that there are no conflicts, concerns or basic self-image issues? Can you be absolutely confident they know they are unconditionally loved by both parents? Some parents are offended when I approach these issues but we need to consider the possibility however painful or distressing. As a child I didn't believe my father accepted or loved me and as a consequence spent a great deal of negative energy and in some cases behaved inappropriately trying to gain his attention, approval and acceptance. All children can gain from this process regardless of their ability or attitudes. There's always room for improvement or change and SleepTalk™ facilitates that change in a simple, non-intrusive manner.

One major benefit I experienced was the sense of empowerment it gave me to assist my own child. Feelings of helplessness were replaced by a sense of strength and purpose, and learning how powerful and important it was to utilise correct terminology when communicating with all members of my world. More importantly as a parent I understood the reasons why it's imperative to always communicate with positive messages. I developed an appreciation and understanding of how inappropriate it is to give mixed messages such as, 'Come here and give me a hug you awful child', or negative suggestions of, 'If you were my first child I'd never have had any more', or, 'You're not as good as your brother are you?' or 'Why are you so hopeless, you won't amount to anything in life.' Statements not meant to harm, we don't mean them, we don't mean to encourage a negative self-belief. SleepTalk™ not only assists our children to have a healthy self-image but empowers us to as well.

The down-line ramifications of change within the family environment can be simply explained as 'cause and effect'. The changes occurring in one member of a family flow through the entire family unit as communication and attitudes alter. As children become more confident, more at ease, they respond differently and in turn that encourages a different response from all members of the family. The benefit of change will affect the eldest child to the youngest family member. As aggravation within a family spreads — it's contagious we all know that — conversely, peace and happiness are contagious as well. Although this process is for children you are actually empowered as parents working with the whole family.

Over the years it has been my pleasure and privilege to work with many families. Some of the workshops which I recorded will enable you to gain an insight into the exciting changes which can take place as you work with this process. This chapter will address some areas which have been identified as primary issues over the years and being able to discuss them further is important. The following workshop dialogues provide a deeper understanding of the SleepTalk™ process.

The conversations were recorded a month after parents had commenced SleepTalk™. Of course names have been changed to protect the privacy of the participants and I acknowledge with thanks the families' permission to share their stories.

Alice's daughter Lyn is nine years of age. There was always major conflict between them, resulting in poor communication and inappropriate behaviour.

Joane: How did you feel conducting SleepTalk™?

Alice: The first week I was anxious because I didn't know if I was doing it right. I wasn't sure if I was doing the stroking right, I wasn't sure when she woke up if I actually had the right brain wave, so I think I spent the first week being anxious and I don't know whether she got anything out of it. But I certainly practised the first week, I settled down and it really became very easy. I'm confident now especially after discussing it with you on the phone. As soon as I entered the room she seemed to wake up and that worried me because I didn't know if she was already in the right brain wave frequency or whether she was waking up or what was actually happening. And you told me that after a while children get used to what you are doing and they transfer automatically.

Joane: They can automatically transfer as soon as they hear any movement and/or sense there is somebody in the room. But what have you done when that has occurred?

Alice: I waited to see whether she actually woke up, but at one point I gave up and I didn't do it for three times in the four weeks because I thought she was awake and I didn't know how to get her back to sleep. And then other times I waited until she was asleep and tried again and then it was all right. Again the other night she sleepwalked. She was standing in front of my bed having quite a normal conversation. The next morning I asked her if she remembered but she had no recollection, so I am never going to be afraid again, even when her eyes are wide open.

Joane: While she was sleepwalking you had the opportunity to use SleepTalk™. You could have said quite easily, 'Lyn just turn around, go back to bed, deep asleep, deep asleep.' Preferably get her back into bed before you say deep sleep, though!

Alice: I didn't know what to do. That was the first time she had done it since I started... I'm far less anxious about it now and it just takes a couple of minutes.

Joane: In terms of change or feedback have you noticed anything, have you noticed any subtle changes at all?

Alice: Yes. There hasn't been a major change, she is a tantrum child, very demanding and hard to cope with. I was anxious and tense all the time with her because I didn't know how to handle her. There has been a subtle shift, I cannot actually put it into words, she is more co-operative, her disposition has mellowed and there are fewer tantrums. She is gentler and when she does have a tantrum she settles down more and the most amazing thing is that she has started apologising for her behaviour. She has never done that before. The other day she said, 'I'm sorry I shouted at you mum.' I was just stunned.

Joane: There is a little angel just trying to get out, isn't it fabulous, and you say she's never apologised?

Alice: No, she's always right and I'm the mean mother! I am very happy with what has been happening and I think if the shift does occur it can only get better. I am going to persevere with this, I think she is on the right track now, I can see the way she approaches her work, there is new confidence ...

Joane: As a mum I experienced enormous changes within myself when I started the SleepTalk™ process. I was able to express my emotions, thoughts and feelings more easily and without fear of rejection.

Alice: I feel I have changed as much as Lyn, just the fact that I feel safe telling her that I love her. I mean, you know that you love her but maybe you don't say it enough. I thought I did, and I think I have really settled down too. I was just an anxious mother. She still has the power to push all the buttons and then I say stupid things. And then I say in my mind, wait until tonight when you are asleep.

Joane: That's brilliant. We'll have to have a chapter in the book titled *Wait until tonight!* If you do happen to say something negative or mistakenly give the impression that you are angry, before sleep just quietly explain it's the behaviour you're rejecting not her. When she commences sleep the emotion and memory of that event will be corrected before it journeys into the subconscious mind as fact.

Alice: I feel much better within myself dealing with my child and I really believe she will continue to improve ... there's some sort of recognition, some sort of integration taking place and there is something in her eyes.

The second workshop dialogue discussed a young girl named Sue. She was experiencing major behavioural problems, aggression and difficulties at kindergarten.

Mum: I have noticed quite a few changes, but I think the first one that comes to mind is probably because it is the most current one. I have been having difficulties with Sue for quite some time. I put her into several childcare centres when I was working and she was more or less expelled. So I was in a situation where I couldn't put her back into childcare until I addressed the difficulties she was having.

A therapist at one stage recommended a centre just for one day a week to get that social interaction with other children. They were having a few difficulties but we were persevering. When I dropped her off this Friday morning they said to me that they were absolutely amazed, she was like a completely different child. They had seen the most incredible changes in behaviour in the past few weeks and they didn't even know that I was doing SleepTalk™. I hadn't had a chance to catch up with them and let them know what I was doing. Sue was a lot more agreeable; it didn't seem to matter what you asked her to do — from something simple like brushing her teeth to something major like cleaning up her toys. Before, she'd been very argumentative and there was nothing you could ask that would be carried out nicely; tantrums were a common occurence. They commented she had been more agreeable, less argumentative, seems to be socialising better with the other children at the centre, sharing, not her usual smash and grab method of getting toys. They said she just seems to be a totally different child. It was at that point that I actually told them that I was doing SleepTalk™.

Joane: What was their reaction?

Mum: They were quite amazed. I mentioned that I have noticed all those qualities at home as well.

Joane: So the changes in behaviour are not just with other people, it's with you as well?

Mum: Definitely, it's just quite amazing. She will come up to me and say, 'I'm sorry' and give me a flower from the garden. I am just finding that Sue has changed regarding the tantrums and things. I am getting a lot more confident with the SleepTalk™ and I think in the first week I was a little bit concerned whether I was getting her at the right stage. I missed one or two evenings of SleepTalk™, only because I couldn't get her to transfer. I seemed to be saying, 'stay asleep, stay asleep' for so long.

Joane: Was the day particularly busy for Sue, was she very tired?

Mum: Yes she did have a very hectic day and was very tired. So I started the SleepTalk™ earlier the next time and it was fine. I have been tuning in to how hectic her day's been and how quickly she falls asleep. If she falls asleep straight away then I might start it earlier.

Joane: Do you think there has been any change within you?

Mum: Oh there has. I think for the first time in a long time I have enjoyed being a mother. I mean I have always loved Sue, there has never been any question about that, but it's nice to be able to take a breath occasionally and to enjoy each other's company and to laugh with her and to enjoy playing with her. That's made me feel a lot happier as I was feeling a little bit of a failure. It was the one thing that I wanted to be good at, being a mum and I felt that I wasn't achieving that.

The third workshop conversation I recorded was with Mary who has two children, a little boy displaying temper tantrums, sibling rivalry, rejection and behavioural problems. Mary's younger daughter suffered from cerebral palsy and co-ordination dysfunction.

Mary: Just at the moment I feel a bit of a failure. I'm using SleepTalk™ with my two children, Alex who is seven and Jane five. After a couple of weeks Alex was high on life, he was just dancing and skipping which was most unusual for him. He had complained of pins and needles in his foot one night, he was just running round the table saying, 'it's getting better, it's getting better'.

I would say that there is a real conflict of negatives and positives in his behaviour and I just feel like I don't know whether I'm coming or going. I just cannot predict what is going to happen. I am sure that's what it is. I can see that one minute he will be fine and the next minute he will be really terrible.

Joane: Internal conflict as the process develops may occur. The negative patterns of behaviour become overwhelmed by the acceptance of positive suggestions. It will settle down.

Mary: You experience the good and get sort of excited. He was different and people noticed it. They would say he's so happy ...

Joane: You mentioned before that Alex had changed his behaviour in the morning. How soon was it before he started coming out of the bedroom skipping and saying, 'I'm happy.

Mary: Within two weeks. But before that he hadn't said 'I love you' to me for about two years. I have always said it to him but he would just never say it. Twice in two weeks he said that. But I could tell he seemed to be thinking, "Is that me speaking, where did that came from?" One time we were having an argument and all of a sudden he wrapped his arms round me and said, 'I love you', and he kisses me a lot ... he sort of jumps on me. He doesn't just come up and hug you.

Joane: Do you think there was a sense of aggression with it?

Mary: Yes, definitely. I would say that the aggression is still there. I'm reacting to him in the same way — we are very similar — but hopefully it will sort itself out.

Joane: Do you remember we discussed the 'Top Hat' process and the positive suggestions being introduced into the subconscious mind alongside the negative beliefs? The continued positive suggestions of SleepTalk™ will eventually become more dominant than the negative. It may cause conflict to start with but eventually the positive suggestions will dominate and dilute the negatives. Tell me about your daughter Jane.

Mary: Jane has just turned five, she is not walking — the cerebral palsy only affects her legs. I started the SleepTalk™ process with her and within a few days she was walking two to three steps holding on to a wall. When I initially started SleepTalk™ she kept saying really negative things such as, "I can't do this, I hate this, and I'm not doing anything you say". But the last couple of days you can see in her face that she thinks she can do things and she walked five steps to me the other day which was brilliant. She was so excited. She'll tackle things now that she wouldn't have before. She's always been very loving though.

Joane: You indicated concern that the extra attention given to Jane as a result of her physical impairment may have caused sibling rivalry with Alex?

Mary: Definitely, Alex was very jealous.

Joane: You have an opportunity with SleepTalk™ to create balance for both your children. You have the next few years to be able to reinforce positive suggestions, giving both children an independent self-image and sense of self worth. It is absolutely fabulous that Jane has started to walk; if she can take two or three steps she can walk 100. That means the muscles will start to develop, her co-ordination and balance will improve and apart from anything else the belief 'I can and will', rather than 'I can't and I won't', will become the dominant desire in her mind. You said that she went to a playground on Friday, tell us about what happened.

Mary: Friday night we went to a fete. There was a playground and she tackled every single piece of playground equipment ... she used the monkey frame because her arms are really strong, but didn't know how she was going to reach it. I was watching her. She was looking at the steps and worked out how to get up there, it was just amazing, she just tried every thing.

Joane: Because Jane's thinking processes have changed, she is now has the belief 'I can' rather than 'I can't ... I'm no good'. She is developing a positive self-image and as a result becoming more confident. She's not using all her energy thinking 'I'm no good'. The compound snowball effect is going to get stronger from all aspects, both physiologically and psychologically.

Mum: I was so excited. She tries to stand and balance in the middle of the room. Anywhere she can stand up and walk, she seems to say, 'I'm going to walk out of here now'.

Joane: Stay with the basics for the moment. Even though it's very tempting to help with the walking and the determination started as a result of the increased confidence and self-image, we have to make sure that the concrete 'Foundation' is really solid. We have to make sure the 'I'm OK' aspect of thinking has been really accepted and become part of Jane's basic belief structure. The major down-line changes as a direct result of SleepTalk™ will continue to occur not just with the children but with the entire family unit.

Definition of madness:
'Doing the same as before and expecting a
different outcome.'
Anon

chapter twelve

The seven principles of thought

SLEEPTALK™ HELPS CHANGE NEGATIVE BELIEF PATTERNS based on fear, to positive belief patterns based on love. Sleeptalk™ is about understanding, accepting and about love. Not the soap opera type of love, not the sexual love that we sometimes automatically relate to, it's about loving ourselves and loving one another without fear, without resentment and without judgement.

Much of life's creative process happens without our conscious knowledge. There are conscious and subconscious forces operating in our life and we need to clearly understand the role of both. Whatever the conscious mind believes, whether the belief is the truth or not, the subconscious mind will dutifully act upon that belief. The subconscious follows any belief either positive or negative with equal impersonal efficiency.

We can consider the conscious mind to be objective — it can judge, weigh up and make conclusions. The subconscious is subjective. The subconscious is sensitive and creative; it is compelled to act upon any thought.

Seven steps of creation

My late husband Jim Goulding said, 'Suggestion is the director of consciousness and autosuggestion is the accepting mechanism of the subconscious.' He further suggested, 'We can place the conscious and subconscious aspects of the mind into seven steps of creation'. You may have heard the saying, 'the mind is a creative instrument.' This is so, and the mind's workings can be summarised in seven steps, showing how the universal life force operates through each human being to bring into reality the concepts we believe in. Let's look at them briefly in order. The life force in all living things gives rise to *conscious thought*. We become aware of the life force movement in our thoughts. Thoughts give rise to *ideas* because pure thought must have some expression. Expression creates *desire.* Once ideas enter the mind they impel us towards our desired goals and we start to search for *conditions* which will assist us to realise the ideas. Once we have determined our conditions, we need to find the *circumstances* where these conditions will be realised becoming the final manifestation, Creation. We create what we imagine to be true when we form a belief, whether it is true or not. As long as the belief is held as truth within the subconscious mind it is accepted as truth.

There are two particularly relevant steps to consider further. The conscious mind is active in step two, where the life force movement becomes thought. The subconscious is prominent at step six, where the conscious mind's desires need a context for their realisation. The saying 'whatever you believe deepest within your heart (subconscious mind) it will be afforded unto you', may now be considered from an alternative perspective.

Become a director of life's circumstances, not a victim

How you perceive your external environment is a reflection of your inner world and its belief systems. To change your circumstances you must first change your attitude to thinking. Be a director of life's circumstances ... not a victim. Identify now who you are — not what you once thought you were. The subconscious only registers emotions and presents their memory to which consciousness then reacts. Therefore, make decisions which are based on sound reasoning of the 'here and now' and be wary of giving energy to thought/feeling reactions which are based upon negative experiences. Don't let these impressions intrude or interfere. SleepTalk™ works because the energy from past negative conditioning is overwhelmed and diluted with positive thoughts.

Do not attempt to remove your memories. Your conditioning was created before you knew who you were and what your mind was capable of. You may have been conditioned by the belief, 'My life is unkind and unpredictable'. Such a person will agree with Murphy's Law — 'whatever can go wrong, will!' Yet this unfortunate view of life is merely the result of conditioning, and conditioning can be changed.

A simple redirection of inner belief systems can create plenty — not poverty; health — not sickness; happiness — not sorrow. You can establish a new system of belief with SleepTalk™ because new directions have the power of conscious creation. This is why the SleepTalk™ process is so powerful yet so simple. You assist your child to establish a positive self-esteem.

Consciousness is always operating, even if it is at an altered level of awareness compared with normal waking consciousness. The subconscious mind is a recording mechanism. It has an impeccable memory of everything that the conscious mind has received and been led to believe. The subconscious mind records all that it receives, and this becomes the accepted 'known'. The subconscious mind does not induce new ideas or create ideas of its own. The subconscious mind constructs a belief structure around what it has been told to believe. It does not, for example, receive one idea as negative, another idea as positive and then decide for itself that it will act upon the positive belief instead of the negative belief.

Anatomy of a mystery

No matter where we live on this planet, we have been trained culturally to accept the belief systems and the ideas of those in authority. These systems stem from ideas and beliefs of those who were *originally* in authority over us. If we are honest with ourselves we will discover that we have superstitions stemming back for perhaps hundreds of years. We have fear systems that came from generations before us. We have prejudices that do not really apply to us — we have accepted the ideas of those in authority over us. These beliefs have separated human beings into various structures, such as nations, races, religions, and professions. The overall separation of one person from another on this planet continues with the prejudices stemming from primitive and ignorant days throughout the course of man's evolution, programming our subconscious minds. Consider the fact that ideas and beliefs accepted by us may not be the truth, but may be an idea of someone else's truth!

The formation of self-identity

Whatever is held as an idea or belief within your subconscious mind will automatically be acted upon by the subconscious, and is bound to manifest outwardly in the circumstances of your life becoming the formation of your self-identity!

From the moment your newborn baby's mind begins to operate, suggestion occurs. In adults, the information presented to the brain goes through a process of conscious and subconscious acceptance. Information may be accepted, rejected or modified to suit existing beliefs. Small children do not have conscious, critical, analytical logic. There is no time or perception in which to develop comparisons such as an adult may. Therefore, a child accepts suggestions readily because the logic aspect of their mind is undeveloped. The conscious mind is always accepting suggestions from its environment and without developed logic transforming suggestions into autosuggestions. These autosuggestions enter the storehouse of memory and become part of a belief system at the subconscious level.

The greatest impact occurs during the first five years of a person's life. During this time, a child is drawing information from those in authority and establishing a basis of self-image for itself, regardless of what the information is. Therefore, a child raised in a negative environment will gain a negative input and as a consequence start life with negative belief systems at the subconscious level. A child raised in a positive environment will receive positive inputs. Children themselves can also innocently contribute to their own negative self-image. Imagine a scene where a very young child is attempting to play with older children. The older child calls for the mother to come to take the younger one away. The older child may say, 'He's no good. He can't play with us. He's too little.' Because of the undeveloped perceptions of the younger child, he is not able to logically analyse that statement. The emotional belief input is that he's just not good enough. He doesn't reason that when he is older he will be as good as the older children. He simply believes he's not good enough and unfortunately the initial belief or event becomes lodged deep within the subconscious memory. The joy and thrill of SleepTalk™ is that you, as the parent or primary carer have the opportunity — in some cases second chance — to make sure that your child has a positive self-esteem.

There is ample evidence to suggest that impressions are being stored in memory before birth. Since this occurs before the memory banks that aid reasoning are developed, such impressions are very powerful. Remember that small children lack the ability to reason as adults do. This is why small children are so impressionable, and why their self-concept is formed so strongly by the age of five and this is one of the reasons why little Michelle developed such a strong belief that she was not OK.

For many years I had the pleasure of assisting people to modify or change their diet, assisting them to cope with alcoholism and the stress related symptoms of hypoglycaemia which in many cases cause depression and perceptual dysfunction. The case of Thomas and John is a great example. Thomas, aged 21, suffered unbearable grief and suicidal tendencies. Thomas had been an only child, and was deeply attached to his father John, who had recently died, and Thomas was unable to bear the pain of this loss.

Thomas and John had always done everything together — fishing, hunting and football. Thomas reasoned that, since he was so much like his father, it was inevitable that he would go the same way as his father.

John had been an alcoholic, prone to bouts of deep depression, suffered from hypoglycaemia, on occasions had violent outbursts against his wife Marge, mother of Thomas. The most serious of these drinking bouts resulted in John breaking Marge's jaw. John was a passive man with very strict moral views when not drinking, but his behaviour when drunk was painfully contrary to his beliefs. Following his attack on his wife he experienced an episode of remorse, withdrawing from all communication. Following the period of withdrawal John became very depressed again, began drinking heavily and died as a result of an overdose of prescribed medication.

Marge said that Thomas had started drinking heavily after his father's funeral, which he had never done before. He had often stated how much he hated drink when he saw how it had changed his father's personality — a man he normally loved and respected. Thomas' drinking bouts had an immediate and drastic effect, causing a replay of his father's drunken behaviour to the point of violence towards his mother. His drinking bouts were often accompanied by threats of suicide, and Marge was at her wits end.

Marge then made a statement that threw the whole situation into clear focus: 'The sad part is that John was not his father's anyway. I married John when I was six months pregnant to another man I had been going with.' She continued to explain, 'Of course, John had known all about this, as the other man had been one of his mates.' Marge believed that John's bouts of drinking and depression had been brought on by his frustration over not being his son's biological father.

After a number of counselling sessions Marge decided that it was appropriate to tell Thomas the truth about his paternity and to counteract the negative autosuggestion, 'I am fated to live out the hopeless life my father lived before me.' Explaining the truth to Thomas about his father had a profound effect on Thomas' mistaken and destructive belief system. He was naturally shocked and upset at first, taking time to accept the simple truth of his birth.

Despite the hurt that Thomas experienced he was able to accept that he was responsible for his own actions. He learned to understand there was no inherent biological reason for him to repeat the misery of the man he had always believed to be his biological father and whom he loved and greatly respected. He realised that he had the freedom to be responsible for his own life circumstances, and did not have to create the destructive circumstances that he had seen in his father's life. He addressed the hypoglycaemia and diet-related problems, took control of his thinking and became master of his own destiny. Thomas' life was changed by the simple realisation that each of us has the power to create the life we desire. As parents we have the unique ability through the process of SleepTalk™ to assist our children to create the life they desire.

The creative mechanism of the mind

The human mind can do nothing but create. The scientific achievements, the architectural, engineering and educational advancements that exist for us on this planet were created by us. They all evolved from the creation, manifestation and implementation of desired ideas.

The silent partner to consciousness

Within the mechanisms of the conscious and subconscious mind, a simple system of cause and effect is working. The subconscious mind is born with its instinct for self-preservation and pleasure, but all the information used in its programming of belief is received from the conscious mind. The memory bank in the subconscious gathers together all the information received during a lifetime and creates from it the subconscious belief system, like a silent partner to consciousness.

The silent partner, the enormously powerful subconscious, has the ability to recreate thought/feeling reactions associated with all it's been taught to believe. The mind can do nothing but create and at the subconscious level cannot decide for itself which thought it should act upon. It has impeccable memory and is stimulated by the present focus of consciousness, whether it be by smell, touch, hearing or vision. It instantly reproduces not only the precise memory of a past event but the thought/feeling reactions produced by the event.

It is estimated that by the time the average human being reaches 50 years of age, this subconscious system of memory recording holds no fewer than 70 trillion pieces of information. We could never build anything like the human mind. If a person lives to a hundred years imagine how many memories their mind must be capable of absorbing and storing. Trillions of pieces of information once stored do not lie dormant, they are always ready to represent their thought/feeling reactions which will influence the attitude of our conscious mind.

How do we go about correcting these situations and taking charge of the subconscious memory from the conscious level? There are many alternative therapies available to us as adults. As parents, we are given the opportunity of knowing how the mechanism works and to utilise the SleepTalk™ process with our children. So to recap … memory becomes stored in the subconscious mind through consciousness. Consciousness receives that which is to be recorded through the stimulation of sight, touch, taste, hearing and smell. The conscious mind receives all stimuli by suggestion from the environment. The power of suggestion causes consciousness to be influenced and finally to make decisions based upon that influence. The following case history documented by Sharon Clark from Queensland demonstrates the creative principle of the mind. She states:

> Some children, such as a little boy aged nine, whom we shall call Hugo, present with multiple problems. His mother reported that he was still wetting the bed, suffered from asthma and his school work was continuing to regress. She indicated that the school had tried to help with medical and psychological assistance but with little success.
>
> The case history indicated a long list of symptoms including both psychological and physiological distress ranging from lack of concentration, poor reading and comprehension, to severe asthma attacks which at times were very frightening and the level of anxiety that he experienced compounded his attacks.
>
> I suggested SleepTalk™ may help and with the support of both parents who were separated at the time the process

commenced. Within two weeks basic feedback was reported and after a further seven days, 'Primary' scripts were implemented. Suggestions from the Confidence/Anxiety script were chosen: 'You are confident, positive and calm' and 'You are relaxed and secure within yourself'. We also added suggestions from the 'Behaviour' group, e.g. 'Life is exciting and fun', and from the 'Asthma' group, 'You breathe freely and easily' and 'Your lungs get stronger and stronger every day in every way'.

Since SleepTalk™ began Hugo has not experienced a major asthma attack. The level of anxiety has continued to reduce with a corresponding improvement in confidence. School counsellors and his teachers have reported major improvement in his school work, especially reading and writing.

The enuresis (bed-wetting) stopped by itself; I did not suggest any specific suggestions to deal with this issue. It appears it was directly linked to his level of anxiety. One major factor may have been the improved relationship between his parents which occurred as a result of their joint involvement in SleepTalk™.

The power of suggestion is the most important thing to understand. Appliances such as recording equipment, light globes, radios etc., are designed to receive the energy of electricity and to operate when it is present; the human mind is designed to accept energy and stimuli from its environment by suggestion. Having received the suggestion, the conscious mind goes through a process of reasoning, deciding whether it will form a belief on the basis of what has been suggested to it or whether it will reject the suggestion. The energy source of consciousness is suggestion, the power by which the highest form of intelligence or energy existing on this planet is influenced. Once the conscious mind accepts a suggestion it immediately transmits its acceptance to the subconscious memory.

Your acceptance or rejection of a suggestion will be based on many things, but primarily the acceptance will be as a result of your previously held beliefs, your self-image, your level of confidence and the nature of your relationship with the person who suggested it to you. The power of the mind is such that it can produce either negative results or just as effectively positive results using the same energy and the same process of thought. It's what you *believe* that the subconscious mind will fulfil, not that which you command or desire.

Human activity has created the world we live in today. Few parts of the globe have escaped our reach, yet we have often created havoc and misery instead of happiness and plenty. By realising that the human mind is a creative instrument we gain the means to put our creativity to positive ends. Once you become aware of the relationship between the conscious and subconscious minds, and of the interplay between desire, conscience and consciousness, you will be in a position to begin making valid and positive life choices. Start right now by using the process of SleepTalk™ and help create a happy and positive world for both you and your family.

chapter thirteen

I love me — well do you?

THE WORD 'LOVE' CAN BE USED TO MEAN THE MOST important feeling we can experience as a human being, and at the same time it can be used to refer to the most trivial of feelings and a whole range of emotions in between. The mother 'loves' her child, the teenage girl 'loves' her puppy dog, and the drunk 'loves' his beer. Love can also be defined as possessive, non-possessive or unconditional. Carl Rogers, the well known psychologist, coined the phrase 'unconditional love' and meant the sort of love which has no conditions attached to it, as opposed to the love which says, 'If you don't do as I say, I won't love you any more.' Now, what has this got to do with SleepTalk™ you ask?

A gift

If you were able to bequeath one, just one and only one gift to your child, what would it be? What would you deem the most important gift of all? If you had that chance, what would you give? Let's go through a few together:

self-esteem	love	prosperity
health	I'm OK	skills
security	knowledge	wealth
equality	creativity	intelligence
quality of life	determination	ability to communicate
beauty	independence	co-ordination
understanding	flexibility	belief in self
acceptance	happiness	confidence
determination	friendship	peace
education	discernment	positive thoughts
love		

Just as an exercise, select a few items from the list that you consider would be necessary as the underpinning emotions of friendship.

My selection included; interaction skills, communication, self-esteem, love, belief in self, confidence, I'm OK, acceptance. You might like to add a few more that you feel are important.

Which emotions or experiences would be necessary to have confidence? You may decide that some of the previous choices may be necessary, as well as including the ones I have chosen; acceptance, co-ordination, security, love, positive thoughts, independence, in my opinion are just a few of the underlying components that I would need to experience confidence.

If we think back to Michelle, do you think she had any of those? Do you think she was confident? For a start she wasn't happy, she didn't have confidence because to have confidence you need to have a belief in yourself, to have self-esteem, to have security, to have an 'I'm OK' self-image and the ability to communicate.

What else do you need to have confidence? Perhaps we might say determination, encouragement and peace of mind. Peace of mind is possible if we have a sense of knowing 'It's OK and I'm OK'. Little Michelle was receiving encouragement some of the time, but were the suggestions being accepted? No, of course they weren't. Too much chatter from the subconscious belief of 'I'm not OK'. How can you be confident if there is no belief in self? How can you be confident if you lack the security of believing that you are loved and lovable?

In 1988 I received the following letter from a most dedicated psychotherapist. The letter not only described in detail a case history regarding SleepTalk™, but also a copy of the diary entries recorded by the child's adoptive mother. It was such a lovely happy ending, that I decided to share the entire story with you.

It's about a delightful young lady aged 11 years who was extremely distressed. The detailed report illustrated how SleepTalk™ can change the energy within the entire family. I have included initial background on Christine so you have an opportunity to appreciate the profound changes that occurred. I acknowledge with thanks the family's permission to share this case history. The names have been altered to respect privacy.

Before beginning SleepTalk™ Christine's anxieties were such that all she seemed to do all her waking hours was worry either about her health or the weather. It nearly drove her and her family mad. She went around looking at the sky — through the windows if indoors — and holding her stomach — because of real or imagined pain. It prevented her from doing school work, playing, going on outings, relaxing at home and being a happy little girl generally. The other children thought her very strange too. Nothing the family said or did seem to relieve her anxieties.

From birth, Christine was a ward of the State and did not experience a permanent home and family for the first five years of her life. She developed many problems including a sense of insecurity, lack of trust, immature speech, behaviour and motor co-ordination problems. She also suffered severe physical abuse. The family became involved with Christine when she was 18 months old — first fostering her then visiting her in her other situations and finally adopting her when she was five. A long, sad, complicated story! I received the following letter and diary entries.

Dear Joane,
Please find enclosed a report on Christine's progress over 12 months ending last December. I am continuing to record her progress this year and things are still on the 'up and up', although at present she is rather anxious and vague at times because her dad is overseas and our four daughters are also not at home very much. She tells me 'our family seems to be breaking up' but she is coping well at school and the teachers are extra happy about the way she has started the year. We have noticed her in the class situation when I help with swimming lessons and she is very much one of the group now and doesn't stand out to the extent she did. Not seeming to need special attention constantly. She certainly seems to be enjoying school and learning new skills. Concentration and co-ordination are really going ahead too. Completed a project by herself in school time — didn't need help or 'standing over' arm movements in swimming — terrific. Relatives noticed great changes after 12 months (not in holidays).

She made lots of progress once she had a settled home but even a secure home and family environment weren't enough to bridge the gaps. Her anxieties and tantrums caused problems which were starting to tear our family apart. We were at a loss to know how to help her, although we had tried various things over the years, including medical and psychological guidance which were all helpful in part but nothing really helped. Because Christine was so anxious, frustrated and distressed, the family seemed to revolve around her moods and every one was getting very uptight. SleepTalk™ began at the end of December 1986. Christine was exactly 11 years old. When we started the SleepTalk™ 'Foundation' script Christine transferred quickly and feedback was recognised after about 7–14 days. As you suggested we continued with the basic script for about three months.

January, February, March 1987 — the following positive things were noted:
Lessening of anxieties, development of independence, little more trusting — coping better when things weren't going 'her way'. After

four weeks of SleepTalk™ she suddenly said one day, 'The fairies talk to me at night. They sound just like my mummy and they say they love me'. Joane — my heart nearly melted!

To us, this was the first major proof that SleepTalk™ was working, although we had thought Christine was calmer and happier. Later that month she started saying things like, 'You love me, don't you!' instead of 'Do you love me?'

April, May, June 1987
As directed we introduced the first 'Primary' suggestions. We chose 'You are safe, secure and loved' from the 'Fear and Anxiety' group of suggestions. We also selected 'you enjoy being with others — you are calm, confident and positive' from the 'Behaviour' group of suggestions. About a month later we noticed feedback that included changes in behaviour and self-image. Less anxiety — responding to re-assurances. Not asking same anxious questions repeatedly. Began looking forward to family outings — without fear of the unknown. Improved interaction with peers, joining in games at school again. Wanting to go and play with friends at their homes. More relaxed and coping better and notable lessening of tantrums.

Wanting to walk to school — alone. Started to ride her bike in the street and went to the library alone. Health fears not a constant problem — no mention of 'tummy pains' over the last two months. School work showed improvement. Story writing becoming more coherent. Homework more efficiently completed and neat — previously needed 'standing over' for every word. Carrying out my instructions better.

Selecting greater variety of reading matter — not just weather books! Involved in more activities and entertaining herself better. Not preoccupied with or talking so much about being burnt by her stepfather and less attention-seeking, coordination has improved, stopped sitting with legs splayed out 'toddler fashion'.

Notes — During the above period we continued to have various problems. She regressed noticeably around Easter, becoming very fearful, anxious and hyperactive. She found coping with holiday situations and change in routine difficult. Too many sweets and chocolate in a short time make her 'cranky'. Her adoptive father went to Japan for two months and a new teacher at school in the same month made her extremely anxious, although the behaviour problems were mainly at school. However, she didn't regress to the stage she was at before beginning the SleepTalk™ program .

July, August, September 1987 Joane, you suggested altering Christine's 'Primary' script again and we implemented the following suggestions. We agreed with your comments and selected from the 'Behaviour' group, e.g. 'Your co-operation and attitude is positive — you are happy to share and communicate with others'. We also included, 'You enjoy school, making friends and learning', from the 'Study' group of suggestions.

The feedback was nearly immediate. Christine became more relaxed generally, rarely getting upset when she couldn't do something or things weren't going her way. Says occasionally 'Oh well, these things happen'. Speech patterns and conversation improved, and visiting relatives commented on Christine's improvement, logical speech, and more mature behaviour. Coping with school holidays the best ever! Lack of routine didn't cause regression.

Keen to try new things and not give up easily. Tasks and activities completed, previously would start many things and give up. Specific improvement noticed in her reading; keenly interested in reading books with chapters rather than pictures. Not talking, writing or reading about weather except on occasions. Her school work showed great progress in comprehension and concentration, completed set work in school, still improving in efficiency with homework.

Jobs at home and school mostly remembered — carried out with minimum fuss! Listens better, more adventurous. Keen to go on variety of outings. No fears expressed, looking forward to school camp — being away from home for five days not bothering her! — visiting friends' houses, even walking off alone, indicating an improved sense of confidence.

Began swimming lessons and is making good progress. Progress noted in physical development — trampoline, throwing and catching skills, balance and keeps telling me she wants to join the Girl Guides!

Weather is no longer a problem at school — still hear about it at home if weather's overcast. Although always reading daily forecast, asking people about weather when talking on phone or visiting.

She seems interested rather than worried! Much more aware of herself in relation to peers, seems to now enjoy the company of other girls.

October, November, December 1987. We implemented the next level of suggestions and selected from the 'Confidence/Anxiety' group. 'Whatever the day brings, you remain calm, positive and in control of your thoughts and emotions' and, 'You are calm relaxed and secure within yourself'. From the 'Goal Achievement' group we selected 'You achieve to the best of your own personal ability'.

It was so great when the feedback began, almost immediately, just like before. More confident, independent, assertive — 'I can do it, I don't need any help — I'll decide'. Preferring to use own ideas — going about things in her own way. Talks about things worrying her when she feels she needs to — displaying greater ingenuity in games and problem solving. Looking after her possessions better — is better organised — doing things without much reminding.

School work: continues to improve in written/listening/comprehension. Greater concentration and she has become far less distractable. Organising school projects by herself and finding out facts independently. School report brought home at end of year shows an overall improvement on the previous year. Reading interests have become wider and more mature. Keen on books about jokes and tricks, appears happier and more relaxed.

Coped quite well with school camp — her increased self-awareness and great need to be noticed has created some social problems because she also likes her peers to play her way, or she doesn't join in. Doesn't cope so well with team games and team situations but starting to show improvement. Excellent progress has been reported with swimming, confidence and co-ordination. This year she actually thought about Christmas gifts for people other than herself! And organised herself with a list and the money! A major improvement!

This brings us to the end of 12 months of SleepTalk™. We, as a family, feel much progress has been made and can see other positive things developing with Christine as we continue into 1988. We are on the whole a much more relaxed and happier family, feeling more positive feeling towards Christine's future.

Of course, there are still problems and some days, for various reasons, we feel we are getting nowhere. However after sharing the positive feedback with you from the diary entries kept on Christine's progress since January 1987, I feel we have come a long way. It has been well worth the nightly commitment. Thank you so much Joane, the world for our daughter is becoming 'happy'.

Every aspect of Christine's emotions and thoughts are interrelated and love, security or a belief that 'I am loved' has become *the* major factor in her world. If you don't feel that you're 'OK' and the rest of the world is somewhat suspect, what does that lead you to believe about yourself? What are you lacking in the belief structure of your self-image? Love. You lack the belief that you are loved and are lovable, you lack the belief that you deserve to be loved. Imagine living within your world feeling that you are not loved, imagine how little Christine felt. Do you think you would be happy if you had received that type of treatment as a child? No, of course you wouldn't. To have peace of mind, you must first know and accept that you are loved and are lovable. It is the basic emotion of life.

Let's have a look at what it feels like to feel 'secure'. Would you feel secure if you felt you weren't loved and didn't love anybody in your world? What about its impact on intelligence? If a child attending school felt unloved, rather than learn they would be more worried thinking about 'I'm not OK, I'm not happy, I'm not equal' Just like Christine when she was at school. What do you think she was thinking, sitting in front of a teacher trying to learn how to read and write? What thoughts, fears, emotions are going to be predominate? 'I'm not OK, I'm not all right. Joe Blow is bigger and better or prettier than me, I can't learn, I'm no good'! Fear and anxiety become the predominant feelings and emotions.

Intellectual intelligence vs emotional intelligence

In Daniel Goleman's excellent book entitled, *Emotional Intelligence — Why it can matter more than IQ*, he talks about the difference between intellectual intelligence and emotional intelligence. So let's look at this important issue. Where do you think intelligence comes from? What would you classify as intelligence? In the past 'intellectual intelligence' has been measured with an IQ test. These days more emphasis is being given to a child's 'emotional intelligence'. For example, identical twins with equal potential to learn are in the same classroom, one twin displaying a confident attitude towards learning and achieving high grades, the other displaying a shy, insecure personality and not achieving or enjoying study.

The confident twin would demonstrate a positive self-image, sitting confidently and happy, as opposed to the shy and insecure twin, who presents with a negative self-image and belief structure, possibly thinking, 'I'm not OK — I'm not as good as my brother; I'm not loveable — you're bigger and better than me'. Is it possible that these factors are affecting the shy twin's learning processes? A secure, confident self-image allows a child to utilise their intellectual intelligence in a more confident manner than a child with a negative self-belief structure. One twin may be thinking, 'I feel great, I don't care whether the cow calves or the cat's got fleas, I'm going to have a good day today'. The other twin would be trying to cope with all the negatives in their world, possibly presenting as less intelligent. Both children receive the same information but interpret it differently, according to their basic self-belief (or lack of) as stored by the subconscious mind.

The two basic emotions in life

Two basic emotions dominate our minds, fear and love. Which one is predominant in your world? Which one do you function from or which emotion dictates your actions throughout the day? Take the case of a very aggressive person or a child who hates everybody and everything. Does the hatred come from love or fear? It certainly isn't from love, and if we work back far enough we will find some deep-seated fear and insecurity. You either operate from an emotion of *love* or an emotion of *fear*. How can you be confident if you are fearful? How can you be happy if you are fearful? Can you look in a mirror and without flinching or looking away say to yourself, 'I love me'? If you can, tune into your feelings at this time; or if that's difficult, try to identify with the emotions, thoughts or feelings that this exercise has provoked in you.

Some years ago a psychologist, Paul Black, shared the following case history with me. Names have been changed to protect privacy.

A six-year-old boy had been prone to sudden and unprovoked aggressive attacks towards other children when playing with them. This problem became apparent when the boy was three, when he broke his leg and was hospitalised. In hospital he spent much of the time fretting. The aggression had increased since that incident.

The parents, whose relationship had been strained, but had now recovered, trained in SleepTalk™ and as a result, the boy made good headway.

We have now identified the primary message that must be accepted by the subconscious of the child's belief. *The belief that they are loved, and are lovable.* The strongest emotion of any child's world is love or fear; positive or negative.

Before we could work with my daughter Michelle it was important to build a concrete belief within the subconscious mind that she was loved and was able to love. All suggestions or ideas accepted or rejected would be assessed from a positive framework of love or a negative framework of fear.

When you buy a home or build a house you would expect that it's built on a solid foundation — certainly not sand. That foundation has to last for the life of the building. It's the same with the thinking process of the subconscious mind. All suggestions which become a part of the belief structure of the person's subconscious mind are assessed, accepted, rejected and valued by a pre-existing structure of belief. If your basic belief structure is negative, then difficulty would be experienced in accepting positive statements because anxiety and fear would be the dominant emotions.

The physiological effects experienced by some children as a result of negative emotions can be very distressing. One such condition is enuresis (bed-wetting), which can be a debilitating problem for so many children. From my experience of employing SleepTalk™

techniques with these children, I believe that in many cases fear is the major cause of enuresis. The following case study came to me from Dr Eileen Feeny, a psychiatrist who has for many years worked with SleepTalk™.

The case involved a six-year-old girl called Ingrid who experienced nocturnal enuresis (bed-wetting at night). She had an older brother of eight who was not experiencing any problems at that time. Ingrid also experienced night terrors, which could have been an associated, or compounding, factor in relation to the enuresis. The longest period of dryness that Ingrid had managed was 4½ weeks whilst her father was in France one year prior to the referral. However, within a week of his return, she was bed-wetting every night. Her mother phoned the Children's Hospital for advice and was told to take her out of nappies, reduce fluids at night and to toilet her. However, these measures did not work, so her mother decided to get further help.

I saw Ingrid with her parents and brother. Ingrid clung to her mother's arm during the session. Both parents had problems disciplining her when she made inappropriate demands or interrupted the conversation.

In her individual play session she was highly anxious about leaving her mother in the waiting room and initially she proved quite difficult to engage in the play therapy. She also reacted with temper tantrums when not allowed her own way. I felt I was fighting a losing battle; her mother also had difficulty separating from Ingrid even briefly and her father was very much on the periphery and hence, not available to help.

I decided to use SleepTalk™ as I was not confident that the more traditional 'Bell and Pad' method would work. We had tried the more traditional approach but on the first night that Ingrid was woken to go to the toilet, she waited until she was back in bed to wet it. Her mother thought it was cruel to get Ingrid to change the sheets and hence did it for her. I knew we had to try something else.

SleepTalk™ involved both parents and gave them a sense of control over what happened. Ingrid's father became more involved and was very enthusiastic about the technique.

After using the basic process for approximately one week, feedback indicated acceptance. We then selected and agreed upon the 'Primary' areas of need using the 'Bed-wetting' group of suggestions.

I saw Ingrid with her parents approximately three weeks after they started the SleepTalk™ process and she appeared to be less clingy, and her parents said she'd not wet the bed for about a week. Six weeks later, things were still going well, and her parents had decided to use the other suggestions — specifically regarding concentration at school — to help their daughter.

The Indigo children

Major behavioural issues that parents and children are trying to cope with now include anxiety and aggression. Many children are being diagnosed as having Attention Deficit Disorder (ADD) or Attention Deficit Hyperactivity Disorder (ADHD). Most diagnosed cases are managed with medication and behaviour modification. There are many books now available on how to manage these conditions. One that I'm particularly impressed with is *The Indigo Children — the new kids have arrived*, by Lee Carroll and Jan Tober.

The treatment for most ADHD-labelled children is drug therapy. In some cases this has assisted, though there are less intrusive and more natural alternatives available. It has also been my experience that diet is a component of behavioural dysfunction. The following case history is an example of the complexities involved with working with these problems.

Sharon Clark, a natural therapist and psychotherapist with a large practice in Queensland, shares the following case history about Jamie, a five year old who presented in June 1995.

1st consultation: Jamie displayed aggressive behaviour which was bordering on self-destructive. After extensive conversations with his mother, it was found that this behaviour was not common in the past. Jamie was also suffering from enuresis and a fear of being left alone. He would not dress or attempt to try to wash himself without mum being present. He was experiencing difficulty in concentrating at school and making friends. The referring doctor's diagnosis was Attention Deficit Disorder, coupled with hyperactivity. Drug therapy, possibly Retinal, was her only recommendation if SleepTalk™ was not successful. The mother had tried psychotherapy and counselling, vitamin and mineral therapy coupled with allergy testing, kinesiology, dietary changes, massage, aromatherapy, etc.

History taking also divulged the family home had been broken into ten months prior. The perpetrator had entered Jamie's bedroom whilst he was asleep. Personal items of Jamie's were stolen and his prize possession, his cat, was killed.

2nd consultation: Basic SleepTalk™ was taught to Jamie's parents. Within seven days Jamie was much improved. His aggression and self-destructive behaviour had subsided.

3rd consultation: Jamie had continued to improve, but still wet the bed and experienced anxiety at being away from his family. The first 'Primary' area of need used 'Bed-wetting', and the suggestions, 'You are safe, secure and loved' from the 'Fear and Anxiety' group were also added.

4th consultation: Jamie was continuing to improve rapidly. His teachers had commented on the improvement in his behaviour and bed-wetting was infrequent. The family doctor thought Jamie's ADD was a misdiagnosis, as he had rapidly improved without drug therapy, whilst his naturopath believed they had finally found the appropriate food combinations.

5th consultation: Bed-wetting had completely stopped and he was washing and dressing himself happily.

6th consultation: Jamie presented as slightly case overconfident. So once again, after discussions with the parents, a change to the process was agreed upon. Suggestions were selected from the 'Behaviour' group: 'You treat others as you would like to be treated' and 'You behave in a socially acceptable manner' were introduced. Jamie is now a well adjusted, normal six year old. Thanks, in my opinion, to SleepTalk™.

The building blocks of suggestion

In 1974 when we began to formulate SleepTalk™ it was necessary to consider Michelle's multiple issues one step at a time. We needed to establish a procedural format identifying the basic structure of belief, and then build on that foundation structure by presenting positive suggestions to compound and build the specific 'truths'.

If we had suddenly started saying to Michelle during the waking hours of her day, 'We love you, you are loved', do you think she would be able to accept those suggestions? No, of course not! We also wanted to give Michelle suggestions that she could talk and walk. We knew she had the ability to talk, the vocal cords were there, and thoughts were there. Even though she had dyspraxia she managed to get her tongue around some words (albeit not very well); and at times could take more than two steps without falling over. Michelle could hold objects, though she sometimes dropped them: her co-ordination of fine motor skills was dysfunctional.

We hypothesised that if she had ability or skills some of the time, if she could do it once, she could do it twice or three times, then we had something to work with. If she had the ability to voice one word then we knew she had the equipment to voice other words. So we developed the 'building blocks of suggestion.' A government psychiatrist, the late Dr Harry Bethune once said to us, 'I would never have thought to work with Michelle in this way. You have managed to create and develop a marvellous, simple, yet dynamic procedure because you didn't know you couldn't'!

SleepTalk™ was developed primarily to assist my daughter Michelle to cope with her intellectual and physical impairments. However SleepTalk™ is relevant for all children. It is for children with difficulties and for children with none. In other words, it is for your child. It is not about 'curing' conditions, but it is about making the most of what 'is'. It is about fertilising your child's mind with the power of the positive, of giving your child the greatest gift of all — an attitude of happiness and confident self-esteem and the message that, no matter what, they are loved and loveable.

Many parents have said to me, 'But my child is normal, there is nothing wrong with them, I don't need to know about SleepTalk™. To this I have replied that I have never met a normal person or child in my life and that every child needs SleepTalk™.

If you can conceive it in your mind
Then it can be brought into the physical world.
Wayne W. Dyer

chapter fourteen

Is my child normal?

THE COLLINS ENGLISH DICTIONARY DEFINES 'abnormal' as not normal, deviating from the usual or typical. Society determines what is considered normal or abnormal behaviour. While one society may express the opinion that drinking is abnormal unacceptable social behaviour, another might believe it to be socially acceptable. In other words, the definition of what constitutes abnormal behaviour is society driven.

According to John Cheetham, a consulting psychologist and director of the Cheetham Consulting Group and founder of the Student Achievement Centre in Melbourne, Australia, to understand how a human being functions we need to be aware of the physical, emotional and intellectual 'worlds' of the individual. Each person's actions are the result of two broad influences: the way they perceive pressures, temptations and pleasures, and the ways they have learned to deal with such influences from their past actions.

Behavioural sciences, the study of human behaviour, are in a way similar to the physical sciences — complex and continually developing as new research is developed. In addition, the emotional intellect is a major factor influencing the individual response or behaviour of a person and these cause-effect relationships are rarely simple. The following information on behaviour is based on the work of John Cheetham. Information regarding his published work or courses is available on the SleepTalk™ website.

What constitutes normal and abnormal behaviour?

When asked what constitutes normal and abnormal behaviour John states that, 'The individual perceptions of people will influence how they see their life and past experiences'. There are many factors that contribute to the development of a human being and to the behavioural patterns that they engage in.

Understanding the dynamics of human behaviour

Human perception also plays a role in answering the question 'What is normal or abnormal'. The way in which an individual's brain will see and interpret something is going to be a determinant of what's normal and what's not normal, what's desirable and what's not desirable. This is a major issue in trying to understand the dynamics of human behaviour. These concepts of *normal* and *abnormal* are ideas that you are going to have to clarify in your own mind, because it is very easy to be persuaded that somebody has a problem, or somebody is abnormal when, in fact, there may not be a problem. Human perception — how we see things — is going to play a role. Two parents may see their child engage in the same behaviour, yet their perceptions may differ, and they may vary in their interpretations of whether it is 'normal' or not.

Conscious memory is selective

Any consideration of what makes a human being do what they do must take into account physical, intellectual, emotional and spiritual factors. Accessing information can be very difficult. Why? Because the conscious mind has its limitations. Memory is selective. Do you remember all the pain in your life? No — and very few people want to! Deaths, tragedies, illness, guilt — but fortunately the conscious mind forgets much of it or pushes it aside, as otherwise we would not be able to function.

Study and research in the physical sciences has shown that simple explanations for complex causes are almost always oversimplifications. People may not consciously recall painful episodes in their lives, yet these episodes may influence what they do today. Internal and external, present and past, factors intertwine to make it difficult to determine what causes what. Apart from assessing whether behaviour is in line with its causes, social and cultural standards determine 'normality' and 'abnormality', not to mention psychological and medical variations in the professional assessment of the child's behaviour, or individual's judgements about 'desirable' or 'undesirable' behaviour.

The following case history came from psychotherapist, Ann Fynmore. She observed that children without 'major concerns' and children who just respond to 'everyday' circumstances can gain a great deal from the SleepTalk™ process.

Six months after the death of her grandfather, nine-year-old Dianne's behaviour deteriorated, and her mother grew concerned. The little girl had become aggressive, especially towards her mother and her appetite was poor. Upon speaking with her she was able to tell me she felt sad and had a heavy feeling in her chest. She had been seeing a psychologist for five months and her parents felt that there was little improvement in her condition.

We discussed the SleepTalk™ process and how it could help reinforce and restore love and security for this girl who was having such difficulty resolving her grief.

Within 18 days of commencing the 'Foundation' process, the mother reported that she felt there was a significant change in Dianne, who was calmer and less aggressive. She was calmer and was not so aggressive with her. Mum felt confident to continue with the process, especially as she had shown the program to the psychologist who said that as it was making a positive change, it would be advisable to keep using it.

Since her grandfather's death Dianne had been coming into

her parents' bed at night, however her mother also reported that Dianne had asked permission to sleep overnight at her cousin's, which was a first!

One month later, although still sad, Dianne was generally happier, sleeping well and her appetite and general health were improving significantly.

Ann shared a second case history about a little girl who was very anxious and easily upset.

I first saw Alice when she was two years old. The first child of professional working parents, she was a very 'clinging' child who slept fitfully at night and needed her mother's constant attention during the day. She became easily upset if she left her sight. The mother then found she was pregnant with a second child — though her joy was somewhat marred by the thought of what effect this would have upon Alice.

We discussed SleepTalk™ and how it would give Alice a sense of security. It would also help her to accept and love the new baby. Both parents became involved in the process and decided to add a 'Primary' area of need suggestion as soon as it was possible.

The process was commenced when the mother was about six months pregnant. The 'Primary' suggestion was selected from 'Sibling Rivalry': 'Your brother loves you — you are very special'. The results were both pleasing for the parents and highly beneficial for the little girl, who responded very quickly.

Later on, Alice was able to visit her mother and new brother in hospital, show a loving interest in her new brother and when visiting hours were over, leave happily with her grandparents. Upon returning home, the mother found that she was able to go shopping and have 'time out' for herself whilst Alice was being minded — without her becoming anxious and upset at being left. The process was resumed several times in the early primary years in time of illness using different specific suggestions from the 'Primary' area of need with equally satisfying results.

The process of encouragement

John Cheetham says that encouragement is a basic human need. People, and especially children, need to feel valued by themselves and others. Encouragement is the process of focussing upon assets and strengths as opposed to focusing upon weaknesses and liabilities. Encouragement reflects an accepting attitude.

Discouragement is based upon the beliefs that one is not adequate to meet life's challenges. Discouraged people are overly concerned with status and prestige. They will often avoid tasks when they fear they will not do well. Some factors that contribute to discouragement are: negative expectation; unreasonably high standards; over-ambition; overemphasis on competition; focusing on mistakes.

We are often 'expert' at finding fault, and focusing on mistakes. Mistakes make many people feel they are failures; their self-worth depends on being right and perfect. Adler (1949) stressed the value of developing the courage to be imperfect. That it's OK to make mistakes, it's OK if we are not perfect. Making mistakes leads to knowledge and growth.

Become accepting. Learn to accept your own imperfections and the imperfections of others. Accept yourself by being willing to evaluate the behaviour, not the person.

Recognise and change irrational beliefs. You will be more encouraging to yourself if you become aware of the irrational beliefs you recite to yourself. Develop the skill of listening to the thoughts you create in your head.

Become aware of language which invites discouragement. The language we use shows our attitudes about ourselves and others. Do not accept: 'I can't ...'

Focus on the positive. If you are going to counteract negative influences in your life, begin by eliminating negative comments. Give yourself a positive comment each day, develop positive expectations about yourself. Start with 'I love me'.

Emphasise contributions, assets and strengths. To feel worthwhile, it is important that you feel your contributions make a difference. Inventory your own assets. Learn to focus on your talents. Concentrate on the things you can do rather than on those you can't.

Focus on effort and improvements. Focus on the process and not the end product. Focus on the pleasure of doing the task, rather than the completion of the task.

Develop a sense of humour. The greatest asset one can have for meeting the challenges of life is a sense of humour. Being able to laugh at oneself takes the sting out of the knocks of life. It helps to place life's events in a context.

Recognise the difference between praise and encouragement. Praise is a verbal reward, emphasising competition; it has to be earned and is awarded for being the best. Praise is a method of controlling people. Praise is an external motivator, focused on the end product or the completion of a task. Encouragement is freely given for effort and improvement. It focuses on assets and strength used in the process of doing tasks. It recognises contribution. Encouragement concentrates on motivating through internal stimulation. It instils faith and belief in the person's capability.

I did my best … isn't it?

As a result of working with my daughter Michelle it was necessary to encourage the belief that her world was safe, and that she develop a sense of acceptance and security, and an attitude of 'I'm OK'. During waking hours my late husband Jim would often say to her, 'Michelle as long as you do your best, that's all that matters, isn't it dear'. She would smile gently and nod her head in agreement; she would say, so proudly, 'I did my best … (nod her head smiling) … isn't it Jim?'

Encouragement uses positive definite strategies to help people feel valued and valuable. Be accepting, assist your child to recognise and change irrational beliefs, reduce the language that invites discouragement, focus on positive aspects and strengths and encourage a sense of humour. By following these guidelines and using SleepTalk™ you will be more able to assist your children to feel happy, confident and loved. They will grow up to be more accepting of themselves, prepared to tackle life in a more confident, happy and responsible manner.

God grant me the serenity
to accept the things I cannot change,
Courage to change the things I can,
and the Wisdom to know the difference.

chapter fifteen

Psycho-nutrition and preventive medicine

IF I HAD KNOWN MORE ABOUT NUTRITION WHEN MICHELLE was younger, it would have made an enormous difference to our collective wellbeing. There is a place for every type of healthcare as far as the wellbeing of our children is concerned.

Nutrition is essential for optimum health

Years of research have established that the minimum Recommended Dietary Allowance (RDA) of vitamins and minerals etc. is completely inadequate for healthy living. It does not take into account environmental, hereditary background or biochemical individuality. The RDA is relevant only for healthy people without stress in their lives, people with an in depth understanding of nutrition for the brain and the physical body, people without 'problems' or genetic weaknesses.

Nutrition for the mind

Many doctors are now embracing the essential importance of

nutrition; that diet affects not only the physical appearance and health, but the mental health as well. Correct nutrition affects our energy levels, our intellectual, emotional and physical well-being. Carl Pfeiffer, PhD, Director of Princeton's Brain Bio Centre in America suggests that learning and practising intelligent nutritional habits should begin in school and that it should be a primary education subject.

What is a balanced diet?

What constitutes a balanced diet? Is it the same for men as for women? How do children's needs differ from adults? What does a pregnant mum need that will ensure a healthy baby? If you're driving a car all day, do you need different nutrients from someone who is digging a garden? How do you know what your mind/body needs for optimum health? Certainly more than the RDA, which was established in the early 1900s, when fresh vegetables were exactly that — fresh from the growers — and meat and dairy food were free from chemicals and growth-enhancing substances.

Preventive medicine has become a major issue with many in the medical and psychological professions recognising the community needs. Carl Pfeiffer states that '… many mental conditions derive from bodily malfunctions — specifically from the absence of vital nutrients in the body. The cause of this may be an abnormal loss of a trace mineral, an inability to keep a normal blood-sugar level, outright poisoning from pollutants or simple adherence to our modern diet of packaged meals, empty-calorie snacks, processed and adulterated foodstuffs.'

He states that, 'The role and function of all known nutrients, from the protein and vitamins with which most will be familiar, to the place and importance of the little known trace elements can make the difference between sickness and health, often between life and death, sanity and mental illness.'

A case history comes to mind regarding Malcolm, a six-year-old boy who suffered from numerous complaints and spent the first few weeks of his life in a humidicrib. Jaundice and whooping cough complicated his condition. This case history was very meaningful for the therapist who was also Malcolm's mother. She shares her story in the hope that it may assist those who have had a similar experience to never give up and to use the power of love.

Malcolm had a brother and sister — he was the middle child. Within the first few days of birth he was diagnosed with gastro-oesophageal reflux, E-coli infection in the umbilicus, RH incompatibility and spent the first few weeks in a humidicrib. Jaundice and whooping cough complicated his condition. By the time Malcolm was six, many professionals had monitored and assessed his condition, which included intellectual as well as physical impairment. His mother, who had an extensive background in early childhood development and psychology, was deeply concerned.

However, medical practitioners and psychological counsellors assured her that Malcolm's lack of discipline, poor concentration, and co-ordination and anxiety — which collectively led to temper tantrums, frustration, increasing aggression and a low self-esteem were 'Nothing to worry about, he will grow out of it!' But Malcolm's condition continued to deteriorate and it became obvious as his speech and co-ordination regressed that a reassessment of his condition was necessary.

Malcolm was diagnosed as having neurofibromatosis, or von Rechlinghausen's Syndrome, a genetic condition characterised by developmental changes in the nervous system, muscles, bones and skin, and marked by the formation of neurofibromas over the entire body, associated with patches of tan pigmentation.

Therapy immediately began and all artificial products including colourings, flavourings, preservatives etc. were eliminated from his diet.

Malcolm's progress was extremely slow and, because six months later he was still on a waiting list for the recommended speech therapy, SleepTalk™ was commenced. Within two months there was a 100% improvement in his speech, compared to his initial assessment. This progress indicated he could accomplish tasks that were impossible just two months earlier. He was able to recite all the days of the week, months of the year and count to 100. He was also able to enjoy and digest his food, his spirits began to lift, and he began to laugh aloud, play more and sleep better. Playground and classroom behaviour improved and the school reported that Malcolm was more co-operative, far less aggressive and less frustrated.

Teacher assessments also reported he was able to sit still and concentrate for at least an hour, answer questions and perform tests involving concepts and ambiguities.

His mother, Paula, a qualified psychologist, has asked me to include the following summary so that you can perhaps have an understanding of what SleepTalk™ really meant to her and to her family:

'Apart from all the positive benefits to the child described herein from SleepTalk™ it is not possible to overlook the benefits for the whole family. The SleepTalk™ for Children process united the family, included the whole family. It took away the negative guilt and blame sometimes inherent in being the parents of an impaired child, and proved to be a rewarding experience, something that the family can do for a child; something that no-one else can do for your child. And ... it works!'

What does psycho-nutrition mean?

Our bodies are complex biochemical units. The quality of the fuel ingested by a human body will determine how well that body functions physically and mentally.

Werbach (1990) states, 'Nutrients work to correct a biochemical imbalance usually more slowly than drugs, although some vitamins such as inositol have a drug-like action. Drugs can have unpleasant side effects, whereas nutrients should be used as the first choice: however, this does not obviate the use of drugs when needed.'

Diet is important to virtually every facet of your life. Good nutrition is not just avoiding bad health and disease. Diet affects your physical appearance, your energy levels, your mental health and general feelings of wellbeing, even your sexuality.

Nutrients are needed to balance the biochemical mix of the brain;

deficiencies develop mainly through stress, diet and hereditary disposition.

Orthomolecular medicine

Psycho-nutrition is sometimes called orthomolecular medicine. Nobel prize winner Linus Pauling described orthomolecular medicine as the provision of proper quantities of nutrients for the individual. More specifically as: 'the preservation of good health and the prevention and treatment of disease by varying the concentrations in the human body of the molecules of substances that are normally present, many of them required for life, such as vitamins, essential amino acids, essential fatty acids and minerals.'

Further to this Pauling states: 'a psychiatrist who refuses to try the methods of orthomolecular psychiatry (nutrition as related to mental health) in addition to his usual therapy in the treatment of his patients is failing in his duty as a physician.'

Enormous efforts have gone into researching the effects of nutrients, or the lack thereof, on the mind. A two year experiment with more than one thousand schizophrenics treated with megavitamin therapy found that 60% of those treated either improved or had total relief from symptoms. The Canadian Schizophrenia Foundation found 85% recovery rate using megavitamin therapy. After further development using a biochemical approach, the Brain Bio-Center in Princeton, New Jersey found 90% recovery. This biochemical approach was found to be more effective, of shorter duration and cheaper than drug therapy.

In 1984 Patrick Holford, one of the world's leading authorities on new approaches to health and nutrition, founded the Institute for Optimum Nutrition in England, one of the most respected training colleges for clinical nutritionists. He also directs the UK Mental Health Project, and since 1997 has written twenty health books, including *The Optimum Nutrition Bible* (which sold over a million copies worldwide), *Natural Highs* and *Six Weeks to Super Health*. For contact details see the SleepTalk™ web page.

But I have a good diet, why do I need vitamins?

People say 'But I have a good diet!' But do they really know what a good diet is? On the other hand, many people feel that their diet is inadequate, but have never read a book or thought about good health. Do they actually know what a good diet is? Is it possible that diet drinks, school tuck shop or fast food meals are contributing to children's lack of self-esteem, confidence, self worth, attitude, health, fitness and achievement? Of course it is! Hypoglycaemia is a malfunction of sugar metabolism and has been linked to hyperactivity in children. Sugar and food allergy play a vital role in these disorders which often go untreated. It's encouraging, therefore, to know that many in the medical profession are starting to recognise the importance of diet and nutrition in relation to general wellness.

A few years ago I received a letter from the mother of a three-year old boy named Harry, illustrating the use of SleepTalk™ in conjunction with corrective nutrition.

Dear Joane,
We wanted to thank you for your help and are happy to report the following for your records. Harry is now just over three years old. He is now a very happy, loving child, eager to learn and help, intelligent and very healthy thanks to combining SleepTalk™ and a well-balanced diet.

About six to eight months ago the story was different. Harry was stressed and run down. He first started by getting frightened of sudden movements or noises, and it just got worse.

There was a new housing estate being established behind our house. If Harry was playing in our backyard and a machine was turned on or a truck revved up, he would immediately run inside to us screaming, 'I don't like the machines — I don't like the men'. He would then cling to us all day and not dare to go outside again.

This continued for a couple of months, then the problems set in — he would not go to bed at night as he was too scared.

Any strangers coming into our home made him anxious, jumpy and uneasy. His health deteriorated. He looked withdrawn and stressed.

It got to the stage where we could not even mow the lawns or use a hammer without Harry becoming hysterical. I'll never forget going to a party one night when a man started carving some meat with an electric knife. Poor Harry became so upset and tense that we had to leave and come home. We saw a child psychologist who suggested we try talking him through each bad situation. This was unsuccessful.

Then we tried SleepTalk™. Within two to three weeks, Harry had improved almost 100%. At about the same time, we began using SleepTalk™ on Harry's sister, Tracey, who is now 1½ years old. Both children have not had any sickness or health problems since we began using SleepTalk™.

It was a very rewarding moment when only after about one week of using SleepTalk™ I said to Harry, '... and was it a bright and happy day today?' and he replied 'Yes and with every day in every way I'm getting better and better!' We also altered the children's diet by cutting out refined foods such as white flour, sugar, artificial additives, etc. and by adding extra vitamin B and C to their diets.

We will always use SleepTalk™ on our children so they know they are loved and safe and they will live their lives without fear and to their fullest potential. Thank you for sharing this process with us.

Once again names have been changed and I acknowledge with thanks the permission granted to cite the case. After all the years that I have been sharing this process with parents, receiving a letter like this just makes my heart sing.

Providing the right fuel for thinking

Just briefly, let's look at the function of the brain. Technically speaking, the brain is a gland because it secretes certain chemicals, but for the sake of this exercise we'll call it an organ. Harmonious logical thought is the function of that organ, however if the fuel that feeds that organ is incorrect, the organ will still continue to function but the function will be impaired.

For example, if you consume alcohol, street or prescribed drugs in an excessive amount you cause great disturbance to the thinking processes. In fact delirium tremors causing perceptual disturbances occur in some alcoholics. But take away the drug or take away the drink and the thinking returns (one would hope) to a level of normality with clear perceptual thought. Nothing wrong with the organ, just the function. If it were the lungs that we were discussing the fuel would be the quality of the air, the correct mixture of oxygen etc. needed for that particular organ to function. If too much smoke or toxic fumes are inhaled the organ would still function, breathing would still occur, but with great difficulty and distress to the person. Eventual collapse of the lungs, as in emphysema could occur. Much like putting low grade fuel or kerosene in a high performance car — there would be nothing wrong with the engine, except for the fuel. These are simplified examples perhaps but easy to understand.

Michael Wilson, a nutrition expert and colleague in Australia, asks, 'When psychotherapy or any talk therapy is being considered, how effective can it be if the very organ (the brain) that needs to communicate and participate in the therapeutic process is malfunctioning or has a perceptual dysfunction?' Psychotherapy may be useful and effective for the release of stress or anxiety, but unlikely to bring about permanent and major relief of personal distress if the mind is not able to operate effectively with perceptual balance. Just treating the behaviour or effect with psychotherapy to manage emotional distress without considering alternatives is not acceptable in today's approach to wellness.

The progressive identification of diet-related conditions and their remedies will allow us to significantly reduce the incidence of physical and mental illness, leaving us with a more healthy and sane society, freeing resources to focus more effectively on the more refractory genetically caused disorders. In other words, we are starting to recognise the importance of preventive, as opposed to curative, medicine.

Believe it and you will see it.
Know it and you'll be it.
The only limits you have
Are the limits you believe.
Wayne W. Dyer

chapter sixteen

Avoidable toxins in our homes

AN APPRECIATION OF NUTRITION AND THE IMPORTANCE it plays in the growth, functioning and behaviour of our children is essential for all parents. Sleeptalk™ assists with the psychological and behavioural aspects of assisting our children, but as parents we must address the physiological issues as well. Elaine Stoeckel is a well known naturopath from Queensland and an accredited SleepTalk™ trainer for many years. Her specific area of interest is nutrition for children, and she has kindly contributed the following chapter.

Elaine outlines children's basic nutritional needs and the relationship of nutrition to behaviour and health, in particular Attention Deficit Disorder (ADD) or Attention Deficit Hypoactivity Disorder (ADHD). You can contact Elaine by visiting the SleepTalk™ web site.

Bodies are approximately 70% water

This is something a lot of parents seem to forget — that water comes first. Our body is made up of approximately 70% water and if we don't maintain that quantity in the system we begin to have problems.

Water is used by the body to transport nutritients to the organs and to remove waste products. It is needed to bathe the cells and for all enzymic and cell functioning to occur. The brain is 80% water so if we are dehydrated there are bigger problems in store.

When we say water we mean **water,** and not the fruit juices, soft drinks, milk or any other beverage with added sugars and chemicals. Water is easily absorbed into the body and bypasses the digestive process that other drinks require.

Contamination of our environment

Nutrition for children is very basic, as it is for all of us. Often problems arise simply due to our environment. Pollution of air, water and food is very common. If we live in an industrialised area we are exposed to greater air pollution levels, which is something we may not be able to do anything about, short of removing ourselves from that area. This is sometimes impractical and unworkable.

Water quality is often unknown; contamination can be accidental, unknown or deliberate. Contaminants can range from fertilisers, pesticides and household run-off to fluoride and chlorine. There is much research and evidence regarding the disastrous effects these additives have on us. There are many more contaminants we need to be aware of.

Contamination of our food

The food market has changed dramatically over the last few decades. We have been so inundated with novel processed food products and fast food outlets, that parents must find it hard to say 'no' to the constant harassment from their child. The advertising is also very cleverly done to offer convenience and to attract the young mind.

If children start the day with commercially packaged 'junk food', followed by a sugar-overloaded fruit flavoured drink or, in some cases, a carbonated soft drink usually with a cola base, it is no wonder there are so many children displaying learning difficulties and behavioural problems such as ADD and ADHD.

Our lifestyle has changed so much that the family breakfast seems to be the thing of the past. Sit-down family meals are few and far between as the hectic daily routine or television takes precedence. Meals in front of the television or on the run have become the norm.

Children tend to 'graze' and the snack foods of choice are often high in fat, sugar and lacking quality mineral and vitamin content. Even low-fat 'health foods' often substitute the fat with sugar, or in the case of 'diet' foods, the substitution is aspartame, an artificial sweetener. The resultant raising and lowering of sugar levels in the bloodstream is detrimental.

When the sugar level is high the person has heaps of energy but when it drops we reach for the sugar to give us a lift. Hence the terms hypoglycaemic and hyperglycaemic. The pancreas works hard to keep the sugar levels constant but with this stop-start action it eventually becomes so overworked that it is virtually 'worn out' and sugar levels run high in the bloodstream.

Hyperactivity, emotional instability and poor concentration can ensue, resulting in learning problems, anxiety and sometimes violence.

When an overload of sugar is taken into the body, and not burnt off as fuel, it is stored in the liver and tissues as glycogen. If the onslaught continues it is eventually converted to fat, leading to obesity.

Our Western diet lacks the fibre to clear some of the sugar from the system. Bread has long been a staple for many cultures yet it is now recognised as an allergen for many people. Is it the extra processing or the added chemicals that cause the problem and creates the reaction to gluten? I believe it is a bit of both. The processing destroys some of the exclusive oils and nutritional value, and artificial additives compound the situation.

We need to eat whole grain or wholemeal breads, definitely not white, even if it has all the goodies added back into it.

And what do we know about milk?

Milk is another staple product that has been altered. Its molecular structure has been changed by being pasteurised and/or homogenised, causing an allergic reaction in many people. So many today are lactose and casein intolerant, and for these people it is best to avoid cow and goat milk altogether. Breast feeding is still best for mother and baby and after this, the child needs to be weaned onto water.

Unfortunately people often defer to an alternative such as soy. Daniel Doerge is a research scientist for the Food and Drug Administration (USA) and an expert on soy. He states that, 'New studies have raised questions over whether soy might increase the risk of breast cancer in some women, affect brain function in men, and lead to hidden developmental abnormalities in infants'.

We tend to initiate health problems when we deviate from the simple natural ways of life. It is advisable to eat raw or lightly cooked fruits and vegetables as much as possible, to eat less meat, and drink plenty of pure water. If you can grow your own fruit and vegetables, or buy 'organic', then the nutritional value has a chance of being much higher. As most of our farming soils are depleted of trace minerals, and other factors are leaching nutrients from our bodies, supplementation is advisable for improved health.

Childhood challenges

When did problems like ADD and ADHD become common amongst our children? It wasn't a term used when I was teaching in the 1960s. Asthma was also a little recognised problem whereas nowadays a large number of children suffer from asthma type conditions.

In 1987 the terms ADD and ADHD were invented by a group of noted psychiatrists. Some of the symptoms of ADD or ADHD, i.e. hyperactivity and learning difficulties, may be associated with allergies, e.g. excessive mucus, rashes, eczema, asthma, bed-wetting and behavioural problems. Today, many people and especially children experience allergic reactions to things in our everyday environment. How many of the behavioural problems may be attributed to sensitivity to smells, chemicals or perfumes? There is little said of this but I know of a child who always felt sick and irritable and finally found out it was his mother's perfume that caused it. Food colourings and preservatives can also cause similar reactions in children, including behavioural problems.

Children exhibiting hyperactivity have altered fatty acid metabolism

By adding the essential fatty acids plus the nutrients pyridoxine (B6), niacin (B3), magnesium and zinc to the diet there has been shown a marked improvement in the immune system of children exhibiting hyperactivity, often resulting in improved behaviour and brain function. The immune system is often low due to the constant onslaught of environmental pollutants, food additives and chemicals, creating deficiencies resulting in poor functioning of the entire mental and physical body, which is then prone to infection and disease. A sick, tired person is unable to concentrate and function to capacity.

Dyslexia

Mental function is often the first thing to be affected by nutritional imbalances and dyslexia is no exception. The copper/zinc ratio needs to be balanced for the right and left brain to function equally. An imbalance can affect psychological functions, including emotions, memory, perception, learning and behaviour. Copper excess associated with hemisphere dominance is seen in children with dyslexia.

Why the imbalance you may ask? The liver and gall bladder are mainly responsible for the excretion of copper through the intestines. Psychotropic drugs, sedatives and tranquillisers will interrupt this elimination process. Children with dyslexia respond well to nutritional supplementation. They may show an improved attention span, better grades, and more emotional stability.

Pyroluria

Vitamin B6 and zinc deficiencies may give rise to a set of symptoms often mistaken as a mental illness, with symptoms including being withdrawn and liking isolation, becoming uncomfortable when set routines are disrupted, constant colds and infections, emotional exhaustion, nail-biting and hypersensitivity to light. Some of these symptoms are very noticeable in children.

Autism

American children still receive up to 20 vaccines in the first two years of life. Australian children are very similar. There is much debate as to the safety of vaccines containing thimerosal. Thimerosal is 50 per cent ethyl mercury by weight, and has been used as a vaccine preservative since the 1930s in the diphtheria-tetanus-pertussis shot, known as D.T.P. It was later added to some vaccines for Hepatitis B and Haemophilus bacteria, which by the early 1990s had become routine immunisations for infants.

The first symptoms of autism often appear between the ages of 12 and 24 months. Is there a correlation? George Lucier, a toxicologist who led a White House review of mercury's dangers states, 'it's very likely that thimerosal has damaged some children.' The latest on mercury suggests that even small amounts of organic mercury could cause neurological impairment to the foetal brain.

In December 1999 the Center for Disease Control (USA) had reason to believe that thimerosal caused developmental delays in some children. One document, for example, records comments made by Robert Brent, a Philadelphia paediatrician who served as a consultant for the thimerosal study:

'The medical-legal findings in this study, causal or not, are horrendous,' he said. 'If an allegation was made that a child's neurobehavioral findings were caused by thimerosal-containing vaccines, you could readily find a junk scientist who would support the claim with a reasonable degree of certainty. But you will not find a scientist with any integrity who would say the reverse with the data that is available.'

Epilepsy, depression, anxiety, suicide

You may ask, what have these conditions got in common? The symptoms of epilepsy, depression, anxiety and suicidal tendencies will often respond favourably to a low protein, high fruit and vegetable diet, eliminating sugar and junk food and taking vitamin and mineral supplementation. Deficiencies of Vitamin B6, zinc, manganese and magnesium are noted in many cases of mental illness. Supplementation, and an avoidance of those foods which are depleted in the essential nutritional components, will assist in a turnaround to better health in quite a short time. For more information visit the web sites listed at the back of this book.

Aspartame and saccharin are 'poisons'

Artificial sweeteners such as aspartame and saccharin are 'poisons' known to cause convulsions and epileptic-type seizures. It has been suggested that aspartame, used in many diet foods and drinks, may be contributing to diseases like multiple sclerosis, epilepsy, brain tumours and blindness. Aspartame is found on the Environmental Protection Agency's 'list of most hazardous chemicals' and yet we have it readily available in a huge range of food and sugar substitutes. Having a very low blood sugar level is as serious as high blood sugar and may also lead to blackouts and coma: all simple sugars should be eliminated and replaced by complex carbohydrates.

Toxic additives — ingredients in our homes known to be human carcinogens

This is an issue affecting our children at an alarming rate, yet there are some simple preventive measures we can take to lessen the risk. Have you noticed how many toxic additives and ingredients are used daily in the home, especially in the bathroom? There are many ingredients known to be human carcinogens i.e. cancer forming. Most people are not aware of this, as there are no warning labels and the facts are not publicised.

Fluoride is used in toothpaste and is swallowed by most children when brushing their teeth. Fluoride accumulates in body tissue, and known effects include convulsions, and changes to the liver, kidneys and respiratory system. Evidence of it being a carcinogen is limited, though according to Dr Ted Spence, author of *The Fluoride Controversy*, it increases the incidence of cancer and tumour growth, interrupts DNA repair and deactivates enzyme activity.

Sodium lauryl sulphate is an ingredient in shampoo, bubble bath, cosmetics soap, and is an eye and skin irritant. It is known to accumulate in the organs especially liver, lungs and brain. Vaginal irritation is also common with girls having bubble baths.

PABA found in sunscreen, is a photon activating chemical that can make susceptible people likely to develop skin cancer.

Propylene glycol which is used in baby wipes, hair care products, cosmetics and lotions is known to cause seizures when ingested by a child, cancer forming in animals, and also teratogenic (affecting the embryo).

Others include the PEG group, DEA, talc, TEA, lanolin, coal tar, aluminium and alcohol. Talc is commonly used in powders and cosmetics and is associated with lung and ovarian cancer. Because of workplace health and safety issues, talc is no longer allowed to be used in some nursing homes.

One in three people now have cancer

Children are affected more than adults by chemical toxicity because of their smaller body weight and, as in the case of bubble bath, increased exposure. I have identified only part of an extensive list of dangerous ingredients used daily by the population in the bathroom and yet there are no warning labels on the containers. The personal care and cosmetic industry is virtually self-regulated.

What can we do?

There are measures that we can take on a daily basis to help ourselves and our families. It is so much easier if we make wise choices and therefore create good habits.

» Ensure a good supply of clean filtered water is available.

» Change our eating habits to include plenty of fresh vegetables and fruits (preferably organic), fibre rich foods, and a small amount of meats and grains. Young children seem to have weaker stomach acids for the successful digestion of meat so give it to them in the form of broths or as a base in soups.

» Supplementation is essential as there is a lack of nutrients in our soils and food chain. Soil depletion was noted as far back as the

1930s. Excessive processing also creates devitalised food, hence the need to supplement with vitamins and essential fatty acids.

» Trace minerals will help to rectify the mineral deficiencies causing so many psychosomatic illnesses. The best source of trace minerals are plant-based colloidal minerals because they are easily absorbed by the body.

» The essential fatty acids are just that — essential for better brain function. Supplementation is advisable from an early age.

» Eliminate junk food and sugar, especially carbonated drinks as they are loaded with sugar.

» Be aware of the preservatives and colourings added to foods and avoid them as these often cause allergic reactions.

» Boycott prepared diet and light foods as they have been heavily processed. Diet foods have added aspartame as a sweetener and light foods have been processed to remove excess fat.

» Get rid of the microwave, or only use it in emergencies: microwaves sterilise the food and change its molecular structure, diminishing nutritional value.

» Children respond quickly to a good tonic or multi-vitamin.

» Buy safe personal-care products. See bibliography for details on S. Epstein's useful book on toxicology.

» Find a dentist that doesn't use amalgam or fluoride. Many dentists have embraced the research showing the dangers of mercury and fluoride.

» Research the pros and cons very carefully before considering vaccinating your children.

» Exercise is so important for the development of motor skills. Children spend a lot of time playing computer games, which has developed their fine motor skills in an amazing way. They also require the larger movements required by sport and other physical activity.

» Relaxation and quiet times are just as important as physical activity and sport. Aromatherapy can aid relaxation; essential oils of chamomile, lavender, tangerine and lemon induce a sense of calmness and clarity.

» Bush Flower essences are powerful, fast acting remedies. Ian White, author of *The Australian Bush Flower Essences* states, 'They are powerful catalysts for helping people help themselves. The essences allow people to turn inwards and understand their own life purpose and direction. They also give people the courage and confidence to follow that plan'.

Parents cannot protect their children from threats they know little or nothing about. So my plea to you as parents is to research the subject for yourselves and get information from all sources possible and then make an educated and responsible decision about your family's health. It really is simple. We make things complicated.

chapter seventeen

SleepTalk™ benefits that last for life

IN THE PREFACE TO THIS BOOK, ALEX BARTSCH DISCUSSED WITH YOU the power of words and the ability of parents to give their child skills to overcome obstacles, recognise opportunities, and to maximise potential for success. Words have the power to build or destroy, comfort or hurt. During the first years of your child's life, when the developing brain undergoes enormous physical changes, it's so important to understand the development that is taking place.

The brain builds its personal 'wiring' system, incorporating a number of programs that facilitate function, survival and development. The practical short and long-term benefits of positive parenting are the safeguards against negative cognitive inoculation.

The SleepTalk™ process is precious and unique. The process needs the commitment of time and effort and I ask you to continue with it each and every evening. In my experience the only time the process hasn't worked is when the personal commitment is lacking. Remember that SleepTalk™ is suitable for all children from infancy to early teenagehood. SleepTalk™ assists and helps normal children to do better; a difficult or troubled child to improve; ADHD children and above all a physically or intellectually disadvantaged child to develop confidence to deal with their world.

Psychologists, medical practitioners and counsellors in clinical practice have used SleepTalk™ successfully since 1974. SleepTalk™ has been researched and verified by a team of psychologists and many successful case histories have been recorded. The precious gift of self-esteem that this process empowers *you* to be able to give *your* child can't be measured by anything in this world. The different case histories provided in this book will enable you to appreciate the wide-ranging circumstances that SleepTalk™ can cover.

As I have mentioned before, intellectually or physically impaired children respond especially well to selected 'Primary' areas of need. Michelle responded to a number of suggestions incorporating movement, balance, speech, her attitude to school and her ability to write and read. Only select and work with one area of need at a time to start with. As you progress in your desired area, you can join two or three suggestions together into one statement. Make sure you give enough time for the process to be accepted before introducing an additional benefit and always keep a diary to record the feedback.

Abreaction or anxiety may be experienced as the new and positive messages are accepted into the subconscious; confusion can occur when positive messages interrupt the 'normal'/established thinking process of your child. But do not stop or become concerned. The subconscious mind will begin to accept the new thoughts and eventually balanced harmony will be achieved if you continue with the SleepTalk™ basic suggestions. SleepTalk™ can also be a major catalyst for change, incorporating and in some cases activating previous assistance and therapy. As a result the suggestions of love and happiness that you give to your child will last for life.

Every child is a magnificent creative being, always learning and always striving for perfection. Your children will achieve in life according to their 'knowing' and accepted 'truths' based on the belief of self-worth and self-image. Use the gift of SleepTalk™ to dynamically improve and protect your child's emotional, intellectual and physical development.

In many ways, the following piece may skim the surface of the reality of this gift. The author is unknown to me. If you know who the writer or publisher is, please share it with me so that I can reference it officially.

NO CHARGE

My little boy came up to me in the kitchen this evening whilst I was fixing dinner and he handed me a piece of paper he'd been writing on. After wiping my hands on my apron, I read it, and this is what it said:

for mowing the lawn $5.00
for making my own bed $1.00
for going to the shop $0.50
for playing with little brother while you shopped $0.25
for taking out the rubbish $1.00
for getting a good report card $5.00
and for raking the yard $2.00

Total Amount Owed........ $14.75

Well, I looked at him standing there expectantly, and a thousand memories flashed through my mind, so I picked up the pen and turned the paper over. This is what I wrote:

for the nine months I carried you, growing inside me
.... NO CHARGE
for the nights I've sat up with you, doctored you, cried for you
.... NO CHARGE
for the time and tears that you've cost through the years there's
.... NO CHARGE
for the nights filled with dread and the worries ahead
.... NO CHARGE
for advice and the knowledge and for wiping your nose there's
.... NO CHARGE
When you add it all up, the full cost of my love is
.... NO CHARGE

Well, when he'd finished reading he had great big tears in his eyes and he looked up at me and said, 'Mum, I really do love you'. Then he took the pen and in great big letters he wrote:

.... PAID IN FULL

When you add it all up, the cost of real love is NO CHARGE.

This last, very simple, yet delightful incident gave me great pleasure. My stepdaughter was one day feeling a little down and was sitting on the sofa with my granddaughter. She was a very sensitive little girl about five years old who had responded very well to SleepTalk™. She went up to her mum and said, 'Never mind, mum... I love you ... It will be a happy day today.'

chapter eighteen

SleepTalk™ research

Cheetham Consulting Group:
John Cheetham: Consulting Psychologist, Australia

Research into the benefits of SleepTalk™

Our organisation was commissioned by Joane Goulding, founder of SleepTalk™ for Children to conduct research into the outcomes and effectiveness of their product, SleepTalk™ for Children. Over a period of some months we studied the history and development of SleepTalk™, collected data on the progress of children involved in it, and received ongoing feedback from parents by way of a self-administered questionnaire.

Our research into the process began with a discussion of SleepTalk™ with its creator Joane Goulding and continued through the briefing of the program's facilitators and support staff. Observations made over this period suggest a long history and much experience has led to the inception of SleepTalk™ for Children.

A major component of our evaluation of SleepTalk™ for Children was an international literature review of the theoretical basis of the process. The outcome of this aspect of our research is presented below.

Research literature supporting SleepTalk™ (Numbers in brackets refer to the number in the reference section of this chapter).

SleepTalk™ is a potentially therapeutic process which enables a parent to interact with their child in a powerful way. It is suggested by its creator that this educational technique enables a child's mind to be focused on positive messages whilst the child is at the correct brain wave frequency of awareness during sleep. Through SleepTalk™, the interaction between parent and child serves to reinforce a sense of security and an ability to cope with daily life.

The closest and most critical bond in life is usually that which exists between a parent and child. For this reason and due to the time and affection shared, parents are usually the primary educators of their children (1, 2, 3, 4, 6, 8, 10). Parents are particularly responsible for the psychological and moral development of the child (2) and the child's intellectual development as well (4, 5). It is possible to develop an environment in which this is facilitated (2). Positive interactions between parents and children have also been found to foster the development of literacy (48). This is perhaps even more the case with children requiring special educational needs (11).

As care givers and educators, parents and guardians are in a unique position to be able to have a positive impact on their children's self-esteem. There are numerous reasons why this is important — certainly people who are confident in themselves have a more enjoyable experience of life (10, 31, 32) and are more likely to be successful (28).

Self-esteem is also a critical factor in learning (4, 30, 33, 41, 42, 46). It reduces fear of failure and increases motivation (25); aids decision-making ability (37); increases children's potential for attempting new or difficult learning tasks (9); has been found to increase levels of academic attainment (7); reduces the likelihood of underachievement as a child or adult (39); and highschool dropout (21). Self-esteem has also been related to workplace performance and career development (12).

Self-esteem and self-comfort have also been linked to creative energy in children and adults in any number of areas (15, 16, 18, 19). Specific studies have found a link between self-esteem and creativity in ballet (18) and poetry, music, painting, sculpture, drama and movement (20). This has also been found in creative analytical, optimising, associative, synthesising and analogical thinking (17).

SleepTalk™ recognises the principle that establishing a strong self-esteem before adolescence is crucial. The challenges of school, family and growing up that teenagers face are difficult to overcome for even the happiest and most content teenagers. For those who do not possess the emotional resilience to press on, depression, isolation and failure may become a way of life. It is important that self-esteem is developed early to ensure that a happy and healthy adolescence follows.

It probably comes as no surprise that adolescents with low self-esteem are more susceptible to peer group pressure (23), alcohol use (22) and substance abuse (23, 40, 43). They are also more likely to become involved in multiple episodes of violence (26).

One way that the bond between child and caregiver can be fostered is by the development of self-esteem through adult-child interaction involved in SleepTalk™. Much research has been conducted in the area of self-esteem and relationships and consensus exists that there is a strong connection between the two (44). In these studies, the strength and stability of loving relationships has been seen to be correlated with the self-esteem of those involved, whether they are children, adolescents or adults. Likewise, a person's perception of their relationships with their partners and others have been found to contribute to self-esteem and happiness (45) at all grade levels.

This love, experienced as a child, can be passed on to the next generation, because children who are loved tend to become loving parents themselves. Likewise, children who have suffered an emotionally deprived upbringing are more likely to construct a similarly loveless environment as parents (34, 35).

The process involved in SleepTalk™ is based on the principles of repetitive learning associated with the sleep state. For many years, repetition has been accepted as an important feature of effective learning (27). More recent studies have suggested that this is true in almost every area of learning (38), including learning whilst asleep (46). Added to this is the simplicity and importance of the message and the reinforcement of the loving bond between caregiver and child.

Few people would deny that quality and refreshing sleep has the power to re-energise people. In addition, an abundance of research has shown that feeling positive before and during sleep can have a number of positive consequences for a child (46, 47). These benefits stem from the child being able to take their optimism or positive mood through the night and into the following day. Feeling positive and secure about oneself can then colour the child's experience of everyday life. Their interpretation of all the incidents and activities in which they are involved is influenced by their feelings about themselves and the world. SleepTalk™ is a technique that seeks to assist children to create a positive attitude towards their world and to approach life with increased belief in themselves.

SleepTalk™ may hold the potential to help children improve their concentration through teaching them to focus their thoughts. For many years, martial arts have been successful in accomplishing this, through making use of the connection between positive experiences, self-esteem and concentration (13). Through self-awareness and exposure to positive messages, concentration can be improved (4, 14).

One of the greatest potential benefits of SleepTalk™, is that it provides a secure context within which a child can safely negotiate emotions. These may consist of fears, anger, loneliness or uncertainty. Whatever the cause of the negative feelings, SleepTalk™ provides a means of reassuring a child of their safety, value and love. This is a much needed outlet. Unresolved issues can be acted out through any number of conscious or unconscious actions or symptoms (24, 29, 36). These can include aggression, bed-wetting, self-isolation or depression.

Although most of the research described above has been conducted over recent years SleepTalk™ is based on principles and understandings which are decades old. The basic concepts of education, repetition and communication of affection are not new.

Our review and consideration of the research outlined above, leads us to believe that SleepTalk™ is based on a wealth of sound theoretical principles. For this reason, one would expect that SleepTalk™ has the potential to be a process of great benefit to many young people and their parents.

Empirical research

With reference to the proposed goals of SleepTalk™, we have designed a questionnaire to empirically measure parents' observations of their children's behaviour, over the duration of the SleepTalk™ process. The questionnaire elicits relevant background information and measures parents' perceptions of their children on 20 indicators of happiness and behaviour, using a five point rating scale. The questionnaire was trialed on a number of parents prior to the commencement of the study.

Parents were required to complete the questionnaire at intervals of three and six months. To our knowledge, this questionnaire was completed by a parent or guardian of every child involved in SleepTalk™.

We analysed the completed questionnaires submitted to us. The mean age of children within the sample was 6½ years, comprising 19 males and 13 females. The 32 completed evaluation forms we received demonstrated a significant improvement in the parents' perception of their children's happiness and behaviour after three months. In other words, over this period of time, the probability that the improvements observed in children who participated in SleepTalk for Children™ would have been due to chance alone, is **less than 0.1%**.

The completed evaluations we received identified improvements in children over a number of areas. These include self-like, enjoyment and participation at school, happiness, relationships with others and confidence. It seems, from our initial research, that parents can reasonably expect their children to have a more enjoyable experience of life, at least in the short-term, as a consequence of their involvement in SleepTalk™ for Children.

Furthermore, it may be that a child need not be 'different' in any way to experience some potential gain from being involved in SleepTalk™. Our experience with the process is that almost any child regardless of personality, intelligence, physical health or pre-disposition, may potentially receive benefit, as a result of the reaffirmation of the child-care giver bond, which SleepTalk™ seems to invoke.

Long-term changes

The research we have conducted in relation to SleepTalk™ has been short-term in nature. The ongoing implications of the process are yet to be seen, except in anecdotal form. We do, however, agree with the creator of the process, when she says that for long lasting changes to occur, completion of the process over the recommended period of time is most likely to yield ongoing benefits.

Conclusion

The evidence supporting SleepTalk™ for Children is consistent. Historical research has demonstrated that the principles, upon which SleepTalk™ is based, are important determinants of behaviour in childhood, adolescence and in some cases, adulthood. Our own empirical study into the effectiveness of SleepTalk™ has brought about promising initial results. The vast majority of parents have observed noticeable changes in their children after relatively short periods of time.

Finally, the parents themselves have also been motivated to provide anecdotal evidence as to the benefits of SleepTalk™. SleepTalk™ seems to be an extremely simple and effective process, which has been seen by parents to benefit many children in their everyday lives and will hopefully continue to do so.

John Cheetham

Consulting Psychologist — Director, Cheetham Consulting Group
Founder of the Student Achievement Centre in Melbourne, Australia

References for the Cheetham Group review:

1. **Parents and school partnerships.** Connors, Lori J.; Epstein, Joyce L. Handbook of parenting, Vol. 4: Applied and practical parenting. (Marc H.Bornstein, Ed), pp. 437-458. Lawrence Erlbaum Associates, Inc, Mahwah, NJ, USA; xxvi, 596 pp. 1995.

2. **Raising other people's kids: A guide for houseparents, foster parents, and direct-care staff.** Camerer, M. C.; Capps, Emerson, Charles C Thomas, Publisher; Springfield, IL, USA; ix, 175 pp. 1995.

3. **Understanding why children in stepfamilies have more learning and behaviour problems than children in nuclear families.** Zill, Nicholas, Stepfamilies: Who benefits? Who does not? (Alan Booth, Judy Dunn, Eds.), pp. 97-106. Lawrence Erlbaum Associates, Inc, Hillsdale, NJ, US; x, 233 pp. 1994.

4. **Learning to learn: Ways to nurture your child's intelligence.** Browne Miller, Angela Insight Books/Plenum Press; New York, NY, USA; xix, 249 pp. 1994.

5. **Intervention to improve cognitive skills of one generation, Introduction to**: Part 1. Beeler, Michael J. The Intergenerational transfer of cognitive skills, Vol.1. Programs, policy, and research isues: Vol.2. Theory and research into cognitive science. Sticht (Ed.) Ablex. Norwood, USA, 1992.

6. **The home environment and school learning: Promoting parental involvement in the education of children.** Kellaghan, Thomas; Sloane, Kathryn; Alvarez, Benjamin; Bloom, Benjamin S. Jossey, Bass Inc, Publishers; San Francisco, CA, USA; xvi, 187 pp. 1993.

7. **Managing learning through group work.** Bennett, Neville. An introduction to teaching: Psychological perspectives. Desforges, Charles (Ed.) Blackwell Publishers Inc. Oxford, UK. 1995.

8. **Sense and nonsense about hothouse children: A practical guide for parents and teachers.** Howe, Michael John Anthony, British Psychological Society; Leicester, England; 121 pp. 1990.

9. **The Courage to Try: Self-Esteem and Learning**. Bernstein, H. E. Learning and Education: Psychoanalytic perspectives. Emotion and behaviour monographs, No.6. Field, Kay: Cohler, Bertram J. & Wool, Glorye. (Ed.) International Universities Press Inc. Madison, USA. 1989.

10. **Teaching children self-discipline... at home and at school: New ways for parents and teachers to build self-control, self-esteem, and self-reliance**. Gordon, Thomas Times Books/Random House, Inc; New York, NY, USA; xxix, 258 pp. 1989.

11. **Parents as teachers of children with special educational needs**. Beveridge, Sally. Cognitive approaches in special education. (David Sugden, Ed.), pp.155-177. Falmer Press/Taylor & Francis, Inc, London, England; 257 pp. 1989.

12. **Workplace basics: The essential skills employers want**. Carnevale, Anthony P: Gainer, Leila J & Meltzer, Ann S. Jossey, Bass Publishers. San Franscisco, USA. 1990.

13. **Psychotherapeutic aspects of the martial arts**. Weiser, Mark; Kutz, Ilan; Kutz, Sue-Jacobson; Weiser, Daniel American Journal of Psychotherapy; 1995 Win Vol 49(1) 118-127.

14. **Evaluation of a metacognitive intervention with cognitive retarded children**. Lauth, Gerhard W. Zeitschrift fur Klinische Psychologie. Forschung und Praxis; 1992 Vol 21(3) 251-261, 1992.

15. **The power motive, self-affect, and creativity**. Fodor, Eugene M.; Greenier, Keegan D. JN: Journal of Research in Personality; 1995 Jun Vol 29(2) 242-252, 1995.

16. **A longitudinal study of correlates of creativity**. Camp, George C. Creativity Research Journal; 1994 Vol 7(2) 125-144, 1994.

17. **Self-esteem: A requisite for creativity**. Shukla, Archana; Sinha, Arvind K. Abhigyan; 1993 Sum Fal Vol 53-60, 1993.

18. **Empathy, self-esteem and other personality factors among junior ballet dancers**. Kalliopuska, Mirja, British Journal of Projective Psychology; 1991 Dec Vol 36(2) 47-61. 1991.

19. An essential interrelationship: Healthy self-esteem and productive creativity. Yau, Cecilia, Journal of Creative Behavior; 1991 Vol 25(2) 154-161, 1991.

20. Creative arts with older people. Special Issue: Creative arts with older people. McMurray, Janice Activities, Adaptation and Aging; 1989 Vol 14(1-2) 138 p, 1989.

21. Early intervention: Linking education and social services with care. Cicchelli, Terry & Baecher, Richard. Staying in school: Partnerships for educational change. Children, youth and change. Sociocultural perspectives. Evans, Ian M: Cicchelli, Terry: Cohen, Marven & Shapiro, Norman P (Ed.) Paul II Brookes Publishing Co. Baltimore, USA, 1995.

22. Self deficits and addiction. Kohut, Heinz The dynamics and treatment of alcoholism: Essential papers. (Jerome D.Levin, Ronna H. Weiss, Eds.), pp. 344-346. Jason Aronson, Inc, Northvale, NJ,USA; vii, 456 pp, 1994.

23. Problem drug use. Hamlin, Moira, Psychology and social issues: A tutorial text. Contemporary psychology series. (Raymond Cochrane, Douglas Carroll, Eds.), pp. 84-94. Falmer Press/Taylor & Francis, Inc, London, England; ix, 227 pp, 1991.

24. The significance of life events as a cause of psychological and physical disorder. Cook, David J. The epidemiology of psychiatric disorders. Cooper (Ed.) John Hopkins University Press. Baltimore, USA, 1987.

25. Making the grade: a self-worth perspective on motivation and school reform. Covington, Martin V. Cambridge University Press. NY, 1992.

26. Self and school success: voices and lore of inner-city students. Farrell, Edwin, William State University of New York Press; Albany, NY, USA; xii, 173 pp. 1994.

26. Skill Acquisition: item specific or item general. Greig, David G. (Unpublished) 1994.

28. Building self-esteem in children (exp. ed.) Berne, Patricia H.; Savary, Louis M. 1996.

29. Recent developments in the study of life events in relation to psychiatric and physical disorders. Harris, T. The epidemiology of psychiatric disorders. Cooper. (Ed.) John Hopkins University Press. Baltimore, USA. 1994.

30. An overview of co-operative learning. Johnson, Roger, T & Johnson, David W. Creativity and collaborative learning: A practical guide to empowering students and teachers. Thousand, Jacqueline S : Villa, Richard A. & Nevin, Ann I. (Eds.) Paul H. Brookes Publishing Co. Baltimore, USA, 1994.

31. Self-esteem: paradoxes and innovations in clinical theory and practice. Bednar, Richard L.; Wells, M. Gawain; Peterson, Scott R. 1989.

32. Making things harder for yourself: pride and joy. Snyder, Mel, L.; Frankel, Arthur 1989.

33. Co-operative learning and students' academic achievement, process skills, learning environment, and self-esteem in tenth grade biology classrooms, Lazarowitz, Reuven & Karsentry, Gabby. Co-operative Learning: Theory and Research. Sharan, Shloro, (Ed.) Praeger Publishers, NY, USA, 1990.

34. Children of alcoholic parents: at risk to experience violence and to develop violent behavior. Rydelius, Per Anders, Children and violence. The child in the family: The monograph series of the International Association for Child and Adolescent Psychiatry and Allied Professions, Vol. 11. (Colette Chiland, J. Gerald Young, Diana Kaplan, Eds.), pp. 72-90. Jason Aronson, Inc, Northvale, NJ, USA; xiii, 217 pp. 1994.

35. Do abused children become abusive parents? Kaufman, J: Zigler, E. Annual progress in child psychiatry and child development, 1988. Chess, S, Thomas, A, Hertzig, M (Eds.) Brunner/Mazel Inc. NY, USA, 1989.

36. Short-term dynamic psychotherapy: Evaluation and technique (2nd ed.) Sifneos, Peter E. Plenum Medical Book Co/Plenum Press; New York, NY, USA; xxiii, 324 pp. 1987.

37. Decision workshops for the improvement of decision-making skills and confidence. Mann, Leon: Beswick, Gery, Allouache, Pierre & Ivey, Mary. Jpurnal of Counselling and Development. 1989, Vol 67(8), 478-481.

38. Optimisation of repetition spacing in the practice of learning. Wozniak, Piotr A.; Gorzelanczyk, Edward J. Acta Neurobiologiae Experimentalis; 1994 Vol 54(1), 59-62 1994.

39. High school underachievers: What do they achieve as adults? McCall, Robert B., Evanh, Cynthia & Kratzer, Lynn. Sage Publications, Inc. Newbury Park, USA, 1992.

40. Adolescents, self-esteem and substance use. Miller, Lynn D, Addictions, concepts and strategies for treatment. Aspen Publishers Inc. Gaithersburg, USA, 1994.

41. Report on learning to learn techniques based on PCP. Nutting, Rosamond. Experimenting with personal construct psychology. Fransella, Fay & Thomas, Laurie (Eds.) Routledge & Kegan Paul, London, UK, 1988.

42. The process of co-operative learning. Putnam, Joanne Wachholz. Creativity and collaborative learning: A practical guide to empowering students and teachers. Thousand, Jacqueline, Villa, Richard, & Nevin, Ann(Eds.) Paul H Brookes Publishing Co. Baltimore, USA, 1994.

43. Self-esteem and drug use. Steffenhagen R.A. Drug and Alcohol Use: Issues and Factors. Einstein, S. (Ed.) Plenum Press, N.Y., USA, 1989.

44. Self-esteem and passionate love relationships. Hatfield, Elaine, The social psychologists: Research adventures. McGraw-Hill series in social psychology. (Gary G. Brannigan, Matthew R. Merrens, Eds.), pp. 129-143. McGraw-Hill Book Company, New York, NY, USA; xx, 279 pp, 1995

45. Adolescent self-esteem and perceived relationships with parents and peers. Blyth, Dale Traeger, Carol, Social networks of children, adolescents, and college students. (Suzanne, Salzinger, John S. Antrobus, Muriel Hammer, Eds.), pp. 171-194. Lawrence. Erlbaum Associates, Inc, Hillsdale, NJ, USA; xiv, 322 pp. 1988

46. Learning, remembering, believing: Enhancing human performance. Druckman, Daniel (Ed); Bjork, Robert A. (Ed) National Academy Press; Washington DC, USA; x, 395 pp. 1994

47. The selective mood regulatory function of dreaming: an update and revision. Kramer, Milton, The functions of dreaming. SUNY series in dream studies. (Alan Moffitt, Milton Kramer, Robert Hoffmann, Eds.), pp. 139-195. State University of New York Press, Albany, NY, USA; x, 610 pp. 1993

48. Families as social context for literacy development. Snow, Catherine, The development of literacy through social interaction. Daiute (Ed.) Jossey-Bass, San Fransisco, USA, 1993.

Researched and prepared by:
David G. Greig BSc (Hons) Dip.Ed. AACE AAPS
Consultant:
John S. Cheetham Pty Ltd, 1996 (Revised 1998)

Bibliography

Allen, Arthur   *The Not-So-Crackpot Autism Theory.* The New
York Times Company.

Anderson, ED   *The impact of suggestions; their effect on children.*
The American Institute of Hypnosis 12, 2, 61-63, 1971.

Bandura, A   *Self-referent thought. A developmental analysis of
self-efficacy.* In Flavel, J.H. Ed., *Social Cognitive
Development, Frontiers and Possible Futures.*
Cambridge University Press, Cambridge, UK, 1981.

Bernstein, Norman
    Diminished People. Little Brown & Co. USA, 1970.

Burns, M.O. and Seligman, M.E.P.
    Explanatory style, helplessness, and depression. In
C.R. Snyder and D.R. Forsyths (Eds.), *Handbook
of Social and Clinical Psychology.* Pergamon Press,
267-284pp, New York, USA, 1991.

Coué, Emil   *Self Mastery Through Conscious Autosuggestion.*
Sun Publishing Co., New Mexico, 1922.

Day, Phillip   *Cancer – Why We're Still Dying To Know The Truth.*
1999.

Day, Phillip   *The Mind Game*, 2002.

Day, Phillip   *The ABC of Disease*, Phillip Day Books Pub:
Credence Publications, Tonbridge, UK, 2003.

Epstein, Samuel S
*Unreasonable Risk. How to Avoid Toxic Ingredients
in Cosmetics and Personal Care Products.*
Pub: Environmental Toxicology, Chicago, Illinois,
USA, 2002.

Gilbert   *Depression: From Psychology to Brain State,*
Lawrence Erlbaum Associates, London, UK, 1984.

Gillham, J.E. & Reivich, K.J.
*Prevention of depressive symptoms in
schoolchildren: A research update.* Psychological
Science, 10, 461-462pp, 1999.

Gillham, J., Reivich, K., Jaycox, L., and Seligman, M.E.P.
*Prevention of depressive symptoms in school
children: Two year follow up.* Psychological
Science, 6, (6), 343-351pp, 1995.

Goleman, D   *Emotional Intelligence: Why it can matter more
than IQ*, Bloomsbury Publishing, London, UK,1996.

Goulding, Jim   *Woman the Carrier of Creation.* McDonald
Bayne, 1990.

Kroger, W.S. & Fezler, W.D.
*Hypnosis and Behaviour Modification. Imagery
Conditioning*, J.B. Lippincott, Philadelphia:, USA,
1976.

Laufer, M.W   *Syndromes of Cerebral Dysfunction And The Relationship Between Psychoses And Mental Retardation in Bernstein,* in Bernstein, Norman R. ed. Diminished People. Boston: Little Brown & Co, 1970.

Miller, Neil Z   *Vaccines – Are they really safe and effective? – A parent's guide to childhood shots.* New Atlantean Press, Santa Fe NM, USA, 1993.

Nolen-Hoeksema, S., Girgus, J., and Seligman, M.E.P. *Predictors and consequences of childhood depressive symptoms.* Journal of Abnormal Psychology, 101 (3), 405-422pp, 1992.

Nolen-Hoeksema, S., Girgus, J., and Seligman, M.E.P. (1986). *Learned helplessness in children: A longitudinal study of depression, achievement, and explanatory style.* Journal of Personality and Social Psychology, 51, 435-442pp.

Osiecki, Henry   *The Physician's Handbook of Clinical Nutrition.* Bioconcepts, 2001.

Peterson, C., Maier, S., and Seligman, M.E.P. (1993). *Learned Helplessness: A Theory for the Age of Personal Control.* Oxford University Press, New York, USA.

Pfeiffer, Carl   *Schizophrenia – ours to conquer.* Bio Communication Press, Witicha Ka, USA, 1970

Sagan, C.   *The Dragons Of Eden: Speculations on the Evolution of Human Intelligence,* Ballantine Books, New York, USA, 1978.

Seligman, M.E.P. and Elder, G. (1985).
Learned helplessness and life-span development. In
A. Sorenson, F. Weinert, L. Sherrod (Eds.), *Human
development and the life course: Multidisciplinary
perspectives.* Hillsdale, N.J.: Erlbaum, 377-427pp.

Seligman, M.E.P. and Peterson, C.
A *learned helplessness perspective on childhood
depression: theory and research.* In M. Rutter,
C.E. Izard, and P. Read (Eds.), *Depression in Young
People: Developmental and Clinical Perspectives.*
Guilford, 223-249pp, New York, USA, 1986.

Seligman, M.E.P.
*Helplessness: On Depression, Development, and
Death.* Second edition. W.H. Freeman, New York,
USA, 1991.

Seligman, M.E.P., Kaslow, N.J., Alloy, L.B., Peterson, C.,
Tanenbaum, R.L., and Abramson, L.Y.
*Attributional style and depressive symptoms among
children.* Journal of Abnormal Psychology, 93, 235-
238pp, 1984.

Seligman, M.E.P., Schulman, P., DeRubeis, R.J., & Hollon, S.D.
*The prevention of depression and anxiety.
Prevention and Treatment,* 1999.

Shatte, A.J., Reivich, K., Gillham, J.E. & Seligman, M.E.P.
Learned Optimism in Children. In C.R. Snyder
(Ed.), *The Psychology of Coping.* Oxford
University Press, UK, 1999.

Watts, David L   *Trace Elements and other Essential Nutrients.*
Trace Elements, Dallas, Texas, USA, 1995.

SLEEPTALK™

Recommended reading and interesting websites

Branden, Nathaniel	*The Six Pillars of Self-Esteem*, Bantam, 1994.
Bays, Brandon	*The Journey™ An Extraordinary Guide for Healing Your Life And Setting Yourself Free.* Element, 2003.
Brighthope, Ian and Maier, Rith	*A Recipe for Health. Building a strong immune system.* McCulloch, 1989.
Brighthope, Ian	*You Can Sleep Soundly Every Night Without Drugs.* Bay Books, N.S.W.
Callahan, Roger and Trubo, Richard	*Tapping The Healer Within. Using Thought Field. Instantly Conquer Your Fears, Anxieties, and Emotional Distress.* Contemporary Books, 2001.
Carroll, Lee and Tober, Jan	*The Indigo Children. The New Kids have arrived.* Hay House, California, USA, 1999.
Cheetham, John	*Teach your child to spell.* Hyland House, 1990 *Grow Up; How to raise an adult by being one yourself.* Wilkins Farago P/L, 2001.

de Haas, Cherie — *Lavender – the most essential oil. Recipes for pampering, good health, nurturing and well-being...naturally*, Pennon Publishing, 2001.

Dyer, Wayne — *What do you really want for your Children.* Hay House, California, USA, 1985. *Staying on the Path.* Hay House, California, USA 1995.

Forward, Susan with Buck, Craig — *Toxic Parents - Overcoming their hurtful legacy and reclaiming your life.* Bantam Books, USA, 1989.

Hay, Louise L — *You Can Heal Your Life.* Specialist Publications. N.S.W. Australia, 1988 *The Power is Within You.* Specialist Publications. N.S.W. Australia, 1991.

Hall, Janet — *How you can be Boss of the Bladder.* Pennon Publishing, Melbourne, Australia, 2003. *Easy Toilet Training.* Pennon Publishing, Melbourne, Australia, 2003.

Haddad, Lois — *SleepTalk™ – A breakthrough technique for helping your child cope with stress and thrive through difficult transitions.* Contemporary Books. Illinois, USA, 1999.

Abram, Hoffer and Tober, Jan — *Putting it all together: The New Orthomolecular Nutrition.* Keats, 1996.

Patrick, Holford — *Optimum Nutrition for the Mind.* Piatkus, 2003.

Lockie, Andrew — *The Family Guide to Homeopathy. The Safe Form of Medicine for the Future.* Hamish Hamilton, 1989.

Matthews, Andrew — *Follow your heart; Finding purpose in your life and Work.* Seashell, Trinity Beach, Australia.

Murphy, Clive — *Empower Yourself. A Practical Guide to Building Self-esteem.* P.O. Box 2421, Wagga Wagga, NSW. 2650, Australia.

Murphy, Clive   *You have the Power.* P.O. Box 2421, Wagga Wagga
                   NSW 2650, Australia.

Pfeiffer, Carl C. Ph.D.,MD.and the Publications Committee of
the Brain Bio Centre
                   *Mental and Elemental Nutrients. A Physician's
                   Guide to Nutrition and Health Care.* Keats, 1975.

Werbach,   *Nutritional Influences on Illness. A
Melvyn R.   sourcebook of Clinical Research.* Keats, 1990.

Weir, Pat, with   *You were born special beautiful and wonderful.
Scandrett, Charlie What Happened?* Weir Knightsbridge and
                   Associates, 1993.

Website addressess and contact details

SleepTalk™   Joane Goulding – www.sleeptalk-children.com

Indigo Children   Jan Tobler   – www.indigoechild.com
                   Lee Carroll

Nutrition   Dr J Mercola   – www.mercola.com
                   Phillip Day   – www.credence.org
                   Elaine Stoeckel – PO.Box 7347 GCMC
                                      Bundall 9726 Aust

Nutritional Products:
Hivita Products: Megavitamin Laboratories – www.hivita.com.au
Efamol Aust. P/L. Australian Contact – www.efamol.com.au
                   – info@efamol.com.au

EEG/Brain Wave   Terry Suckling
                   – www.thehypnotherapycentre.com

Psychology   John Cheetham – Student Achievement Centre
                   – www.studentachievement.com.au

                   Alex Bartsch – Zenith Professional Development
                   – www.zenithpd.com.au

Training organisations – contact details

National College of Traditional Medicine – www.nctm.com.au
Contact: Sandi Rogers

Born to be Free – www.TeyaInc.com
Contact: Teya Antonio-Wright

Alpha Training – www.08002succeed.co.nz
Contact: Roger Saxalby

Trinity Academy (nutrition) – trinityacademy@hotmail.com
Contact: David Kliese

Index